RE REALLY GHOSTS?

QUESTIONS about Angels, the Supernatural, and the Psychic Friends Network

JAMES N. WATKINS

THE WHY FILES

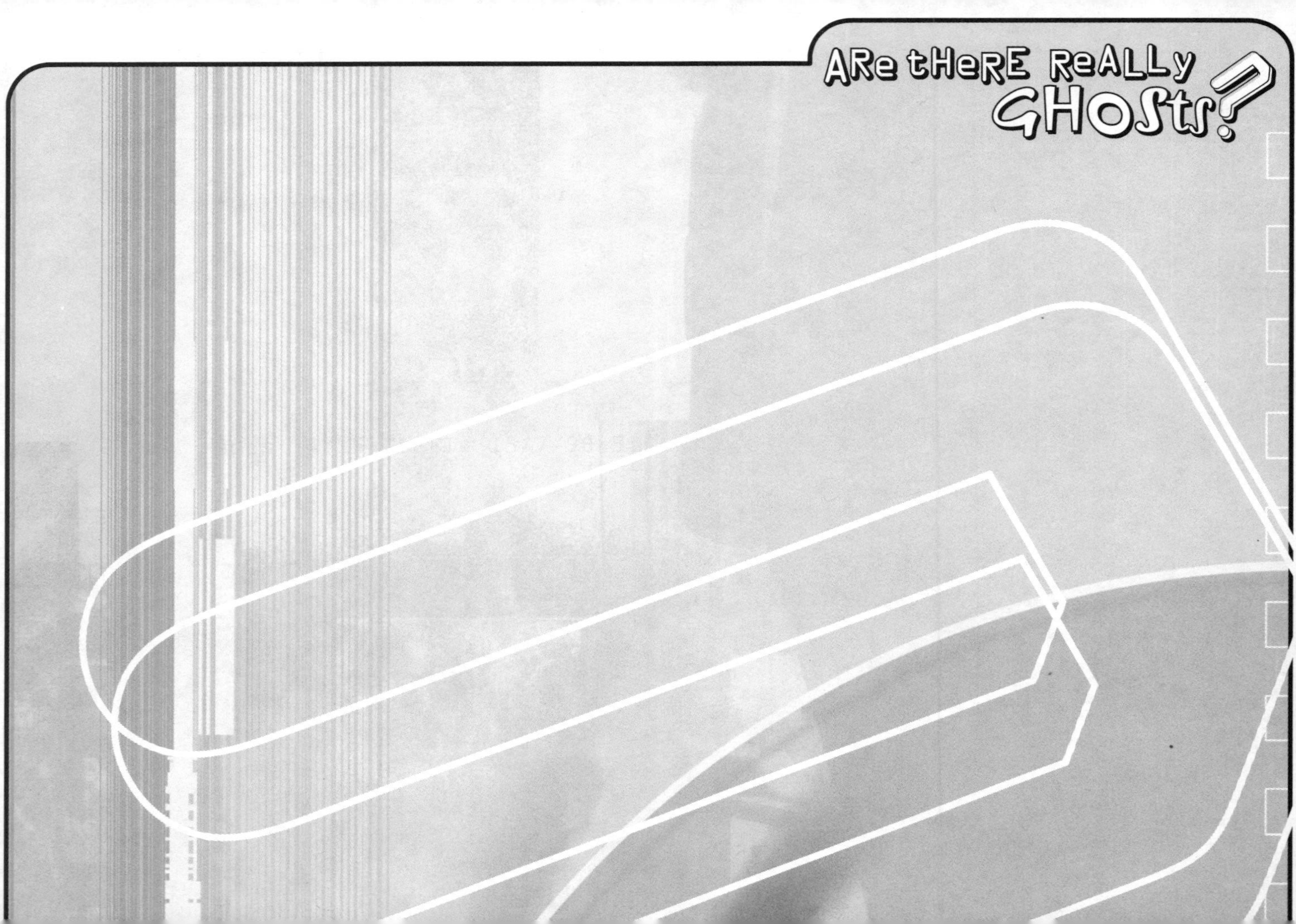
ARe tHeRE ReALLy GHOSts?

about Angels, the Supernatural, and the Psychic Friends Network

JAMES N. WATKINS

To my super wife, Lois, a true patron of the arts.

Who else would support a

struggling writer

and

speaker

who doesn't have a "real" job?

The Why Files

When Can I Start Dating?
Questions about Love, Sex, and a Cure for Zits

Is There Really Life after Death?
Questions about School Shootings, Grief, and Coming Back as a Gerbil

Are There Really Ghosts?
Questions about Angels, the Supernatural, and the Psychic Friends Network

Cover design by Karol Bergdolt. Interior design by Melissa Jarnagin.

Published by Concordia Publishing House
3558 S. Jefferson Avenue, St. Louis, MO 63118-3968
Manufactured in the United States of America

Library of Congress Cataloging-in-Publication Data

Watkins, James, 1952-

Are there really ghosts? : questions about angels, the supernatural, and the psychic friends network / James N. Watkins.
p. cm. — (The why files)
Includes bibliographical references and index.
ISBN 0-570-05248-3
1. Occultism--Religious aspects--Christianity. 2. Christian teenagers--Religious life. I. Title. II. Series.
BR115.03 W38 2000
261. 5´13--dc21

00-012243

1 2 3 4 5 6 7 8 9 10 10 09 08 07 06 05 04 03 02 01

CONTENTS

Foreword

I have been privileged to know Jim Watkins since he was a high school student. He attended my Youth for Christ Campus Life Club in Battle Creek, Michigan, during those days.

I have watched him grow from a struggling writer to an accomplished wordsmith who has kept a strong commitment to helping students both identify and understand the critical issues of their generation.

Jim's ability to address difficult and controversial subjects facing the current youth culture is second to none. He creatively formats and positions insights, values, and biblical principles in a way that captures the imagination. His writings provide solid answers in a language understood by the student world.

This book strategically provides answers to critical questions consistently being raised by today's students and at the same time most often not answered by the church.

The mystical and spiritual world is one of the most talked about topics among the current generation of students. Because there are so many false teachings out there, *Are There Really Ghosts?* is a must-read for every student and every adult who works with them.

I thank God for Jim Watkins and his ability to clearly present biblical answers to difficult questions.

Dr. Richard Wynn
President of Emerging Young Leaders
Former President of Youth for Christ

Acknowledgments

Thanks to 1,000 teens from northern Indiana.
for their honest questions.
Great questions! Wow!

Thanks to Dick Wynn for writing the foreword
and for having such a profound effect on my life
as Campus Life director while I was in high school.
(I hope I'm not the reason you're no longer with YFC!)

Thanks to my editor Rachel Hoyer,
who worked with Concordia Publishing House when we started this project. You made me look good!

And most of all, thanks to my family—
Lois, Faith, and Paul—
for allowing me to hog the computer for the last three months.

Introduction to The Why Files

Jim: Excuse me. I'm taking a survey. Could you answer a few questions?

Jim: Sure, that sounds kind of interesting ... wait a minute! You can't interview me—I'm you ... I mean, you're me!

Jim: Look, Jim, I'm just doing my job.

Jim: You can't interview you, I'm me, I mean, you're me ...

Jim: Just look in the mirror and answer my first question: What do you think is the number one issue on the minds of young people today?

Jim: This is ridiculous!

Jim: Just answer the question.

Jim: Okay, fine. I just finished surveying more than 1,000 junior and senior high students on three subjects: adolescence, death, and the supernatural. I distributed the surveys in public and private schools, in rural as well as urban ...

Jim: Okay, okay, so you surveyed a bunch of people. Just answer the question: What is the number one issue on the minds of young people today?

Jim: Dating issues were the most asked questions on the adolescence survey, "Is there really life after death?" topped the death survey, and questions about God and ghosts topped our supernatural survey.

Jim: So how did you pick these three topics?

Jim: While I was editor of a teen magazine, I kept looking for articles on love and sexuality, but I never found any that honestly dealt with the issues, so I started writing them myself. Those articles eventually turned into three books on sex—everything from abortion to zits!

Then my book editor asked me to write about death, which, surprisingly, our surveys showed was of even more interest to young people than sex! So I've covered everything from grief to out-of-body experiences.

Finally, after you've spent 10 years writing about sex and death, the only bigger subject is the universe itself: God and the whole supernatural realm of angels, demons, ghosts, psychic powers, etc., etc.

Jim: And what makes you think you have the answers to all those questions?

Jim: Well, I've worked as an author and youth speaker all my professional life, and I lived in a girls' dorm for six years, and ...

Jim: You lived in a girls' dorm?!

Jim: I knew interviewing myself was a bad idea!

Jim: So?

Jim: My wife was resident director at Indiana Wesleyan University while I worked with students on campus. What I was trying to say is that I've learned as much working with teens and young people as they've ever learned from me. And one of the most important lessons I've learned is that simple answers to complex questions don't satisfy young people.

Jim: So you don't have a lot of answers?

Jim: Well, I've tried to take young people and their questions seriously, plus I've done an awful lot of research to find the answers.

Jim: So you *do* have all the answers?

Jim: No! I don't have all the answers, but I try to share some thoughts that will help young people think about these three big subjects. I realize that each person is different, so it's hard to give an answer that satisfies everyone. That's why I try to give a general answer when young people write or e-mail questions. But I usually close with something like this:

> **I'm glad my writing has helped you deal with some of these issues, but paper and ink are not enough. I wish**

I could sit down and talk with you face-to-face over a Diet Pepsi. Books, articles, letters, and websites can be helpful, but those can't address your one-of-a-kind situation.

You need a real, live, flesh-and-blood person to give you emotional, social, and spiritual support as well as guidance to make the right choices. I'd encourage you to talk to an adult you trust, such as a member of the clergy, a school counselor, or a youth worker.

Jim: So if your readers want to get in touch with you, how do they do that?

Jim: I love to hear from readers! They can write me c/o Concordia Publishing House, Book Development Department, 3558 South Jefferson Avenue, St. Louis, MO 63118-3968 or e-mail me at whyfiles@jameswatkins.com.

We've also set up a website with links to the resources mentioned in this book series. There are additional resources and up-to-the-minute information on sex, death, and the supernatural at www.jameswatkins.com.

Jim: Anything else in closing?

Jim: I'd like to thank each reader for buying this book. I hope the time we spend together through these pages will be not only informative, but encouraging as well. And, of course, I'd love them to tell all their friends about these three books. Or, better yet, buy a copy of all three books for all of their friends!

Jim: Well, thanks for your time. I'll let you get back to your writing.

Jim: You're welcome ... I think.

Introduction

I have in my right hand, direct from my home office, today's Top Ten list: What are the top 10 questions teens ask about the supernatural?

10. Can ghosts really haunt people?
9. Can demons really possess your body?
8. Are there really witches?
7. How can God be everywhere at one time?
6. Are there really UFOs?
5. Where did God come from?
4. Is there really a supernatural world?
3. What exactly is the Holy Spirit?
2. Are there really aliens from outer space?

And the number one response when we asked nearly 1,000 junior and senior high students, "What's a question you have about the supernatural?"

1. Are there really ghosts?

Other questions in the top 20 included: How did God come to be? When we die, do we become angels? What did Jesus look like? and Can you ever see God?

So how do you answer questions about angels, aliens, ghosts, and God? Let's begin with how we answer any question about the unknown.

I introduced you to my high school's very own "alien," Rob Holt*, in book two of this series, *Is There Really Life after Death*. He always wore cotton in his ears to filter out the "earth frequencies." He claimed they were higher pitched than those of his native planet. Rob refused to participate in swimming during phys. ed. (His "high-voltage energy field" would turn us mere humans into boiled crabs if he got into the pool with us.)

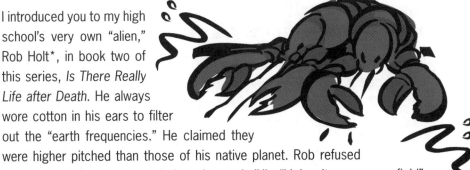

But the biggest difference was Rob's god, **"Kosgro McOrlo Excelsior."** He, she, or it lived in a gold gift box in his locker. And for just 25 cents, classmates could take a peek at this god in a box.

I've lost touch with this unique student. Had Rob lost touch with reality? There are three possibilities.

1. Rob was no **alien**—and he knew it. The whole "Kosgro McOrlo Excelsior" routine was a scam to rip off students' lunch money. Instead of a court-appointed psychiatrist, Rob deserved an Oscar for "Best Portrayal of an Alien by a High School Student"—or at least a warning from the Better Business Bureau.
2. Rob was no alien—but he really thought he was. In this case, in-patient treatment at the state **mental hospital** probably would be in order.
3. Rob really was an alien. The rest of us were merely **ignorant earthlings** who were unaware of Rob's remarkable powers.

* Not his real name

How can you tell if stories about the supernatural are true?

Simply because something is hard to believe doesn't make it false. We've all experienced events that cause us to exclaim, "You're not gonna believe what happened!" Say, for instance, you sink a basketball from half court. How can others know it's true? There are several questions that relate to the incredible basket—and Rob.

1. Is Rob a **credible** person? Can we believe what he says? Can people believe you when you say you sank a basketball from half court?
2. Are Rob's stories **consistent** with one another? Are they consistent with other stories of extraterrestrials? In the case of the basketball shot, do you tell the same story, with the same details, each time?
3. Can other people **verify** Rob's story? Are there reliable eyewitnesses to his supernatural powers? Were your friends or the coach watching when you sank the basket?
4. Do Rob's "history" and "observations" of the universe **agree** with historical or scientific evidence? Your basket can't be "scientifically" proven because that would demand that you could readily repeat the feat each and every time under the same conditions (you probably can't). But you could have "historical" proof (eyewitnesses, videotape, or an article in the school paper) that it did happen at one point in time. Others can go to the school and see the basketball hoop and ball.

If there are major flaws in Rob's story, then it's doubtful that he's really a space-traveling follower of Kosgro McOrlo Excelsior. But if his story stands up to reasonable investigation, then we need to give it serious consideration.

Is there really a supernatural world?

The same kinds of questions need to be asked of those who claim they have been abducted by aliens, seen ghosts, are witches, have seen into the future, have talked to the dead, and even those who believe in the God of the Bible. We'll also examine Ouija boards (chapter 5); channeling, crystals, New Age beliefs, "out-of-body experiences," and tarot cards (chapter 8); as well as other **supernatural phenomenon**. (Because many of these issues overlap with others, I've added an index to this book.)

I believe you'll find that truth is "out there." It simply may be that you can't see it with your physical eyes. For instance, we can only "see" a small portion of the light spectrum from violet to red. We can't see radio, TV, or microwave signals, yet we wouldn't have broadcast music, video, or Internet service without them. They're very real but beyond our ability to see. We can "hear" sounds only within the range of 15 hertz to 20,000 hertz, yet dogs can easily hear higher pitches than humans. And some animals have a sense of smell **100 times** more sensitive than our own.

So it's rather arrogant to claim, "If I can't see it, hear it, smell it, taste it, or touch it, it's not real." Yet some people—including otherwise brilliant scientists—refuse to believe anything they can't explain. That's like saying, "Because I can't figure out how David Copperfield floated in midair or made the Statue of Liberty disappear, I don't believe in the famous illusionist."

Admittedly, the supernatural has gotten some bad press. Just stroll through the grocery store checkout lane to see the tabloids' headlines:

Toothless Vampire
Forced to Raid Blood Banks!

Devil's Triangle Cruise Sends Two Couples Back to 1960

Baby Born with Angel Wings! Flies off to Heaven!

Bat Boy on the Loose!
Half-Human Monster Flees Research Center and Goes on Terror Rampage

Satan's Face Seen in Storms Worldwide

Werewolf Kills 47!

I Had Big Foot's Son!

They're Here!
Extraterrestrials Landing on Earth—And Making Contact with Humans!

U.S. Scientists Bring Mummy Back to Life!
Shocked Doc Blows Whistle on Top Secret Experiment

Hey, I'm not making these up! They're all in the September 7, 1999, "Collector's Edition" of the *Weekly World News*. Really!

Scientists, who are a bit more analytical and skeptical than tabloid reporters, are beginning to catch a glimpse of the supernatural. Albert Einstein's theory of relativity claims that when one reaches the speed of light, one becomes infinite in time and space. The Bible, in 1 John 1:5, says that light is one of God's characteristics. So if God is light, then we would expect Him to be both infinite in time and space—which is exactly what the Bible teaches.

I heard that Jesus' new body had 27 dimensions. Is that true?

Science is also investigating the possibility of multiple dimensions of time and space. (Theoretical physicist John Schwartz claims there are up to 26 dimensions, while Ed Willten and Nathan Seiberg are more conservative, speculating that there are 10 dimensions in our universe.) A being that is not bound by the dimensions of height, width, and depth could do amazing things, such as disappear and reappear in another location, as well as pass through solid doors and walls. And without the restriction of time, such a being could live forever. Hmmm. Does any of that sound like the stories of Jesus Christ after He was resurrected from the dead?

So before we write off the supernatural as unscientific and totally unbelievable, let's take a careful look at the evidence. Keep in mind that astrology was once considered a "science." And for centuries, scientists believed the sun revolved around a flat earth.

It was Augustine, a fourth-century church leader, and Thomas Aquinas, a 13th-century theologian, who speculated that the world wasn't flat, but spherical. Aquinas used both math and physics, as well as observations of the spherical shape of the earth from lunar eclipses, to make his case. The scientists, not people of faith, were the original "Flat Earth-ers"! Scientists also taught that the sun revolved around the earth until a Catholic priest named **Copernicus** proved otherwise during the 1500s.

It was Jesus who said, “You will know the truth, and the truth will set you free” (John 8:32). And the apostle Paul who wrote, “Test everything” (1 Thessalonians 5:21).

So grab your soft drink and settle back in your favorite chair as we search for the truth. It is out there—and in here!

> Dear friend, I pray that you may enjoy good health and that all may go well with you, even as your soul is getting along well. (3 John 2)

Jim Watkins

Part ONE

How Much Supernatural Stuff Can Be Proven?

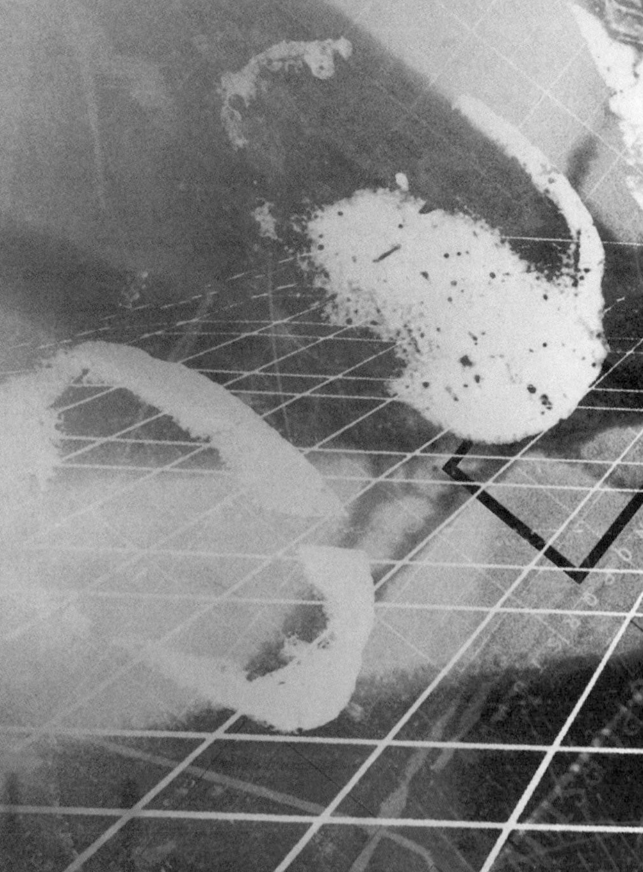

CHAPTER

1 Are There Really UFOs?

Yes! Next question, please.

Okay, maybe I need to explain that answer.

In ninth-grade debate class, one of our topics was "Do UFOs exist?" I ended up on the affirmative side. There were lots of books and theories, but nothing we felt would hold up in a debate. Finally, we devised a **devious plan**.

In just 15 seconds, we would prove the existence of unidentified flying objects.

I stood up to begin our presentation. Suddenly, from the back of the room, a friend lobbed a wad of aluminum foil at the panel. My partner quickly grabbed it and stuffed it under his jacket.

"Do you know what that was?" I asked in my best district attorney voice. The negative team shrugged their shoulders in unison.

"Then you will agree that you could not identify it?" They nodded their heads.

"And will you agree that it did **fly** through the air?" Scowling, they again agreed.

"And will you agree that it indeed was an object?"

Heads reluctantly nodded a third time.

"Then you have just agreed that unidentified flying objects do exist."

Despite the high-pitched whining of "unfair," the debate was over. The teacher merely smirked and went into a lecture on the importance of clearly defining the terms of debate.

So there is no question that there are "unidentified flying objects." The Air Force's "Project Blue Book" and the Mutual Unidentified Flying Object Network have thoroughly documented their existence. The question, then, is *What are UFOs?*

Are **UFOs** manned (or creatured) by alien life-forms from other planets? Or are they merely secret government aircraft, weather balloons, swamp gas, or the observers' elevated blood-alcohol levels? Or are they something else that is beyond scientific explanation?

Does the Bible mention other planets or life-forms? Did God create aliens?

If there is life on other planets, the Bible teaches that God created it:

> For this is what the LORD says—He who created the heavens, He is God; He who fashioned and made the earth, He founded it; He did not create it to be empty, but formed it to be inhabited—He says: "I am the LORD, and there is no other." (Isaiah 45:18)

> For by Him all things were created: things in heaven and on earth, visible and invisible, whether thrones or powers or rulers or authorities; all things were created by Him and for Him. (Colossians 1:16)

A few Bible commentators believe Jesus spoke of life on other planets when He said, "I have other sheep that are not of this sheep pen" (John 10:16). More likely, Jesus was speaking of the Gentile (or non-Jewish) "flock," not ETs.

The Bible does describe the priest Ezekiel's sighting of a heavenly craft.[1]

> I looked, and I saw a windstorm coming out of the north—an immense cloud with flashing lightning and surrounded by brilliant light. The center of the fire looked like glowing metal, and in the fire was what looked like four living creatures. In appearance their form was that of a man, but each of them had four faces and four wings. … The appearance of the living creatures was like burning coals of fire or like torches. Fire moved back and forth among the creatures; it was bright, and lightning flashed out of it. The creatures sped back and forth like flashes of lightning. As I looked at the living creatures, I saw a wheel on the ground beside each creature with its four faces. This was the appearance and structure of the wheels: They sparkled like chrysolite, and all four looked alike. Each appeared to be made like a wheel intersecting a wheel. As they moved, they would go in any one of the four directions the creatures faced; the wheels did not turn about as the creatures went. Their rims were high and awesome, and all four rims were full of eyes all around. When the living creatures moved, the wheels beside them moved; and when the living creatures rose from the ground, the wheels also rose. … Spread out above the heads of the living creatures was what looked like an expanse, sparkling like ice, and awesome. (Ezekiel 1:4-6, 13-19, 22)

The Journal of the Royal Meteorological Society records the log of Captain F. W. Banner aboard the *Lady of the Lake*. According to the **captain's log** of March 22, 1870, Banner and his crew noted "a cloud of circular form, with an included semicircle divided into four parts, the central dividing shaft beginning at the center of the circle and extending far outward, and then curving backward." The "cloud" was gray, much lower than the other clouds, and traveling against the wind. "For half an hour this form was visible."

More than a century later, nearly 10 million Americans, including former President Jimmy Carter, have testified to similar sights: an object with a circular shape, a gray metallic color, and the ability to travel against the wind, which would seemingly rule out the ever-popular "weather balloon" explanation. And the 1870 sighting couldn't be pinned on the usual list of suspects of airplane landing lights, satellites, or the Goodyear blimp.

The most famous UFO incident occurred more than 50 years ago in **Roswell**, New Mexico. Stories of the alleged crashed spaceship and injured aliens have spawned an entire fleet of books and websites, major motion pictures, TV series, and specials. (Who can forget *The X-Files, Alien Autopsy, Independence Day,* and even *Roswell*?) It also has made the residents of the New Mexico town rich and famous.

The myths, conspiracy theories, and government double-speak have created a story so complex and contradictory that fact and fiction are impossible to sort out! We do know that on July 7, 1947, Mac Brazel, a rancher who lived near Roswell, called the local sheriff to report some unearthly looking debris strewn across a pasture. The sheriff called the brass at the Roswell Air Army Field, who dispatched **intelligence officers** to analyze the wreckage. The next day, in the *Roswell Daily Record*, an Air Force official was quoted as saying the government had taken possession of "a flying saucer."

On July 8, Brigadier General Roger Ramey of the Air Force retracted the previous statement. The debris was simply "an ordinary weather balloon." The government recently admitted it was conducting—at that very time and place—a top-secret project code-named "Mogul." Instruments to detect evidence of Soviet nuclear testing were being airlifted by craft resembling weather balloons.

A few weeks before the Roswell incident, Kenneth Arnold had been flying his private plane. He spotted nine glowing objects near Mt. Rainier in Washington state, traveling "well over 1,000 mph." The businessman told Associated Press reporter Bill Bequette that the "crescent-shaped objects ... behaved like a rock or saucer skipping across water." Newspapers across the country dubbed the objects as "flying saucers."

During the three weeks between Arnold's sighting and the Roswell wreckage, hundreds of flying saucers were reported in Canada and the United States. Was it all the talk—and **paranoia**—of flying saucers that caused Brazel to report the debris? He had found the debris, and left it undisturbed, nearly a month *before* reporting it at the height of the UFO frenzy.

Are there really aliens from outer space?

And what about the aliens that were reportedly discovered? Were they spirited away by the Air Force to the mysterious "Area 51"? Curiously, eyewitnesses never mentioned alien bodies at the 1947 crash site until 1989—42 years later. The witnesses themselves described the "aliens": They "looked like twins," as "dummies or bodies or something" looking like "plastic dolls ... with no hair."[2]

The Air Force admits dropping 67 crash-test dummies from "skyhook" balloons launched from nearby Holloman Air Force Base between 1954 and 1959. The huge balloons generated numerous UFO reports, even when the locals were told in advance of the flights.

Bernard Gildenberg (USAF, retired) was involved in the *Project Blue Book* and *Roswell Report: Case Closed* government reports. He believes that the Roswell "myth" has grown through the years and incorporated new details, such as the alien bodies, along the way. "It appears that events strung out over a number of years in the distant past may indeed have been cobbled together to form the basis of a supposed single event."[3]

Have people really met aliens?

So virtually all UFO sightings can be explained away. But what about "encounters of the third kind" where humans actually meet aliens and, in some cases, are taken up into **SPACESHIPS?** That should be proof positive!

Susan Blackmore teaches in the Department of Psychology at the University of the West of England. She's studied the similarities among those who claim to have been abducted.

Most encountered a "gray," a being about four feet tall, with a long body and neck, a large head, and huge black, slanted, almond-shaped eyes. Grays usually have no hair and often only three fingers on each hand. The similarity of the descriptions would seem to prove that the witnesses are truthful.

Are people really abducted by aliens?

Dr. Blackmore also found that most abductions don't occur on deserted back roads like we see in the movies and TV. The majority occur at night while people are home, safe in bed. Here's a description of a typical encounter.

> There is an intense white or blue light, a buzzing or humming sound, anxiety or fear, and the sense of an unexplained presence. A craft with flashing lights is seen and the person is transported or "floated" into it. Once inside the craft, the person may be subjected to various medical procedures, often involving the removal of eggs or sperm and the implantation of a small object in the nose or elsewhere. Communication with the aliens is usually by telepathy. The abductee feels helpless and often restrained, or partially or completely paralyzed.[4]

The similarities in the descriptions of what the aliens look like and how they abduct people seem to make a believable case. And for those of us who are naturally cynical or skeptical, remember, just because something is hard to believe, it isn't necessarily false. But there do appear to be some logical—and scientific—explanations.

For instance, if we study the size and shape of aliens throughout the 20th century, we find that the grays are a recent phenomenon. Robotic aliens were popular early in the century, while the "Buck Rogers" type with ray guns were often seen in mid-century. Glenn G. Sparks of the Department of Communications at Purdue University believes this shift occurred because television and movies shape our visions of the "unknown." No one reported seeing grays before they were introduced on the **SILVER SCREEN!**

Many researchers believe they have a logical explanation for the similarity in abductee experiences as well.

First, Dr. Blackmore doesn't believe abductees have lost touch with reality. **Abductees** were no less intelligent than a control group (who hadn't reported an abduction). They did, however, believe more strongly in alien visitations.

And according to Robert Baker's research, "self-proclaimed 'alien abductees' exhibited an array of unusual traits that indicated they had **fantasy-prone** personalities." For example, Baker analyzed Whitley Strieber, author of *Communion*. This best-selling book is the "true story" of Strieber's own alleged abduction. (And the cover art popularized the big-eyed gray look.)

Baker believes Strieber to be "a classic example of the [fantasy-prone personality] genre." Symptoms include being easily hypnotized, having vivid memories, and experiencing hypnopompic hallucinations ("waking dreams"). He also was "a writer of occult and highly imaginative novels" and exhibited other characteristics of fantasy proneness. Another study by Bartholomew and Basterfield in 1988 drew similar conclusions.[5]

So here's how Dr. Blackmore explains it.

> **Abductions are elaborations of sleep paralysis, in which a person is apparently able to hear and see and feel perfectly awake, but cannot move.**
>
> **Imagine the following scenario: A woman wakes in the night with a strong sense that someone or something is in the room. She tries to move but finds she is completely paralyzed except her eyes. She sees strange lights, hears buzzing or humming sounds, and feels a vibration in the bed. If she knows about sleep paralysis, she will recognize it instantly, but most people do not. So what is she going to think? I suggest that, if she has watched TV programs about abductions or read about them, she may begin to think of aliens. And in this borderline sleep state, the imagined alien will seem extremely real. This alone may be enough to create the conviction of having been abducted. Hypnosis could make the memories of this real experience (but not real abduction) completely convincing.[6]**

Okay, I had never heard of "sleep paralysis" until I began researching alien abductions. But according to the good doctor, 46 percent of adults and 34 percent of children have experienced it. And like "out-of-body" experiences discussed in the second book of this series, the event—whether real or not—is *believed* to be real.

True UFO believers, however, are convinced all this is just another government cover-up. Based on denials from President Nixon concerning the Watergate break-in to President Clinton's denial of having "a sexual relationship with that woman—Miss Lewinsky," the government's credibility is slightly above that of a used-car salesperson.

If UFOs don't exist, why is there so much proof?

One of the first official government reports on UFOs was the 600-page *Unidentified Flying Objects—Project Grudge, Technical Report No. 102-AC-49/15-100* released in December 1949. *Project Blue Book* cataloged UFO reports from 1949 until its final report on December 17, 1969.

More than 90 percent of all reported UFOs, upon investigation, turned out to be **IFOs**: Identified Flying Objects. Everything from distant airplane landing lights, the planet Venus, ball lightning, and weather balloons to other natural astronomical and meteorological phenomena have been reported as UFOs.

The scientific study of UFOs continues with the J. Allen Hynek Center for UFO Studies and **MUFON**, the Mutual Unidentified Flying Object Network. (You can visit their sites at this book's website at www.jameswatkins.com.)

Are there really aliens from space?

Alan Hale, one of the discoverers of the Hale-Bopp comet, would love to meet an alien and take a ride in a spaceship. But he has some serious concerns.

1. Extraordinary claims require extraordinary evidence.
   Therefore, in order for me to accept it, you must produce extraordinary evidence. What might this evidence be? I want the aliens visible front and center, where there can be no reasonable doubt as to their existence. Stories about "lights" or "things" in the sky do not impress me, especially when such reports come from people who have no idea of the vast array of natural and manmade phenomena that are visible in the sky if one would only take the time to look.
2. The burden of proof is on the positive.
   If you are making an extraordinary claim, the burden is on you to produce the extraordinary evidence to prove that you are correct; the

burden is not on me to prove that you are wrong. Furthermore, you must prove your case by providing the direct and compelling evidence for it; you can't prove it by eliminating a few token explanations and then crying, "Well, what else can it be?"

3. **If one is confronted with a series of phenomena for which there exists more than one viable explanation, one should choose the simplest explanation which fits all the observed facts.**

   It is an undeniable fact that many people have seen, or at least claimed to see, objects in the sky and on the ground for which they have no explanation. But it is also an undeniable fact that people can make mistakes about their observations. It is an undeniable fact that reports can come from people who are unaware of the various phenomena that are visible in the sky and from people who are not equipped or trained at making reliable scientific observations. It is an undeniable fact that a person's preconceived notions and expectations can affect his/her observations. It is an undeniable fact that some people will lie and will create hoaxes for any one of various reasons. Taking all these undeniable facts together, the simplest explanation—to me, anyway—for the UFO phenomenon is that every report is either a hoax or is a mistake of some sort. If this explanation is incorrect, then you have to increase the sphere of undeniable facts; and for this, see points 1) and 2) above.[7]

So is there life on other planets and, if so, are these life-forms visiting our planet? It is possible, but there is little credible evidence to support this theory.

Yes! Next question, please.

Okay, okay. You won't let me get away with simple answers, will you? Yes, there are people who claim to be witches. But they're not the "Wicked Witch of the West" or even the "Sabrina, the Teenaged Witch" variety. And forget about broom-jockey

CHAPTER

Are There Really Witches? 2

Harry Potter and his Hogwarts School of Witchcraft and Wizardry.

According to the English Oxford dictionary, WITCHCRAFT is a Celtic word describing people who worship nature and claim to draw their power and knowledge from it. *Wicce* (pronounced *wick-kay*) designates a female witch while *wicca* (pronounced *wick-kah*) describes a male witch. (Whatever you do, don't call a male witch a *warlock*. That's a Scottish word meaning "oath breaker" or "traitor." And those practicing witchcraft also are very sensitive about people confusing stage magic with their brand of *magick*, spelled with an extra *k*.)

Witchcraft, wicca, and neo-pagan beliefs are founded on a "nature-based belief system." Those who follow the "old religion" believe in one god, while many others believe in local gods and goddesses. Most believe that an ultimate power does not rule nature, but is nature itself. Wicces, wiccas, and neo-pagans don't like to be confused with New Agers, who often incorporate the idea of the Judeo/Christian God into their smorgasbord of beliefs.

According to *Power of the Witch* by Laurie Cabot,

> **The earth and all living things share the same life-force. They are composed of patterns of intelligence, of knowledge, and of divinity. All life is a web. We are woven into it as sisters and brothers of All. Witches need to be grounded in both worlds and awake to their responsibilities for both worlds. It is only by being responsible human beings that we can be responsible Witches and only responsible Witches will survive.**[8]

Some followers believe in an afterlife spent in "another plane of existence" known as Summerland, Avalon, Valhalla, or simply the "Other Side." There, they believe, they will be reunited with friends and family.

As far as **stereotypes,** witches and wiccans don't wear black robes to go shopping or walk the dog. They do, however, believe black absorbs "light information" and helps them become "more receptive to psychic impressions and energies."

Are hexes and spells real?

Witches do use spells, which they describe as "a thought, a projection, or a prayer." Witchcraft books point out that the word *spell* does not imply doing evil or harm. In fact, the witch's code or *Rede* is to "harm none." They believe that doing evil or harming someone is against all ethical and moral laws.

Many witches and wiccans believe in some form of reincarnation. Most neo-pagans also believe they will be punished threefold by the laws of karma or as a result of "cause and effect." (So much for witches turning people into toads and frogs.)

Witches do use magic, I mean, *magick* wands and amulets, which are used in "healing and directing energy."

Witches also have several important symbols. For witches, the pentacle or pentagram is a symbol for protection and universal wisdom. The five-pointed star drawn with a continuous line, and sometimes shown inside a circle, represents the human body and the earth protected by the goddess/god force. The pentacle is viewed as a symbol for Universal Wisdom.

Christians believe prayer is a petition to God; however, most pagans believe that the divine is present in everything, including themselves. They believe, then, that spells "are the channeling of our own divine selves, our own energies, to create the change." Contrary to TV's self-centered Sabrina, SPELLS are not to be used for personal gain, such as causing a spell-ee to fall in love with the spell-er. Most wiccans believe that anything manipulative, which goes against the free will of another, is wrong.

Do witches worship the devil?

Most witches resist the stereotype that they worship Satan. In fact, neo-pagans reject the whole idea of a Satan, devil, or any all-evil deity. They also argue that the pentagram, or five-pointed star, is not satanic. They believe the five points correspond to the elements air, earth, fire, and water with the top point corresponding to "Spirit." The pentagram in a circle may also represent a human with his or her legs and arms outstretched, surrounded by universal wisdom or the goddess.

What do witches do out there in the woods?

Witches meet in covens, small groups of no more than 13 people, usually on the night of a full moon. They also celebrate eight holidays, or Sabbats, evenly spaced throughout the year.

Two such sabbats are Samhain on Halloween and Yule on the night of the winter solstice. Each Sabbat has its own symbols and significance. For example, Samhain is the witches' New Year's Eve, which represents death and rebirth.

Each meeting begins with the creation of a sacred space, called the "casting of a circle." Goddesses and gods are summoned and are considered to be physically present. By **chanting** or dancing, the participants raise a "cone of power" up from the circle, which leads to a trance state designed to induce visions and spiritual insights. Rumors of ritual orgies arise from neo-pagans' acceptance of nudity, premarital sex, and homosexuality since sex is seen as "the generative force in nature."

Can you be a Christian witch?

Both the Old and New Testaments of the Bible speak against practicing witchcraft, casting spells, and worshiping nature.

While witches are very tolerant of most religious beliefs (except Christianity), God says in His Word that one cannot be involved in pagan practices and, at the same time, be pleasing to God.

> Let no one be found among you who ... practices divination or sorcery, interprets omens, engages in witchcraft, or casts spells, or who is a medium or spiritist or who consults the dead. Anyone who does these things is detestable to the LORD, and because of these detestable practices the LORD your God will drive out those nations before you. (Deuteronomy 18:10-12)

> The acts of the sinful nature are obvious: sexual immorality, impurity and debauchery; idolatry and *witchcraft;* ... . I warn you, as I did before, that those who live like this will not inherit the kingdom of God. (Galatians 5:19-21, italics mine)

> Although they claimed to be wise, they became fools and exchanged the glory of the immortal God for images made to look like mortal man and birds and animals and reptiles. ... They exchanged the truth of God for a lie, and worshiped and served created things rather than the Creator—who is forever praised. Amen. (Romans 1:22-23, 25)

So to answer the first question in this chapter, yes, there are witches. But they don't fly on broomsticks or invite Hansel and Gretel over for lunch.

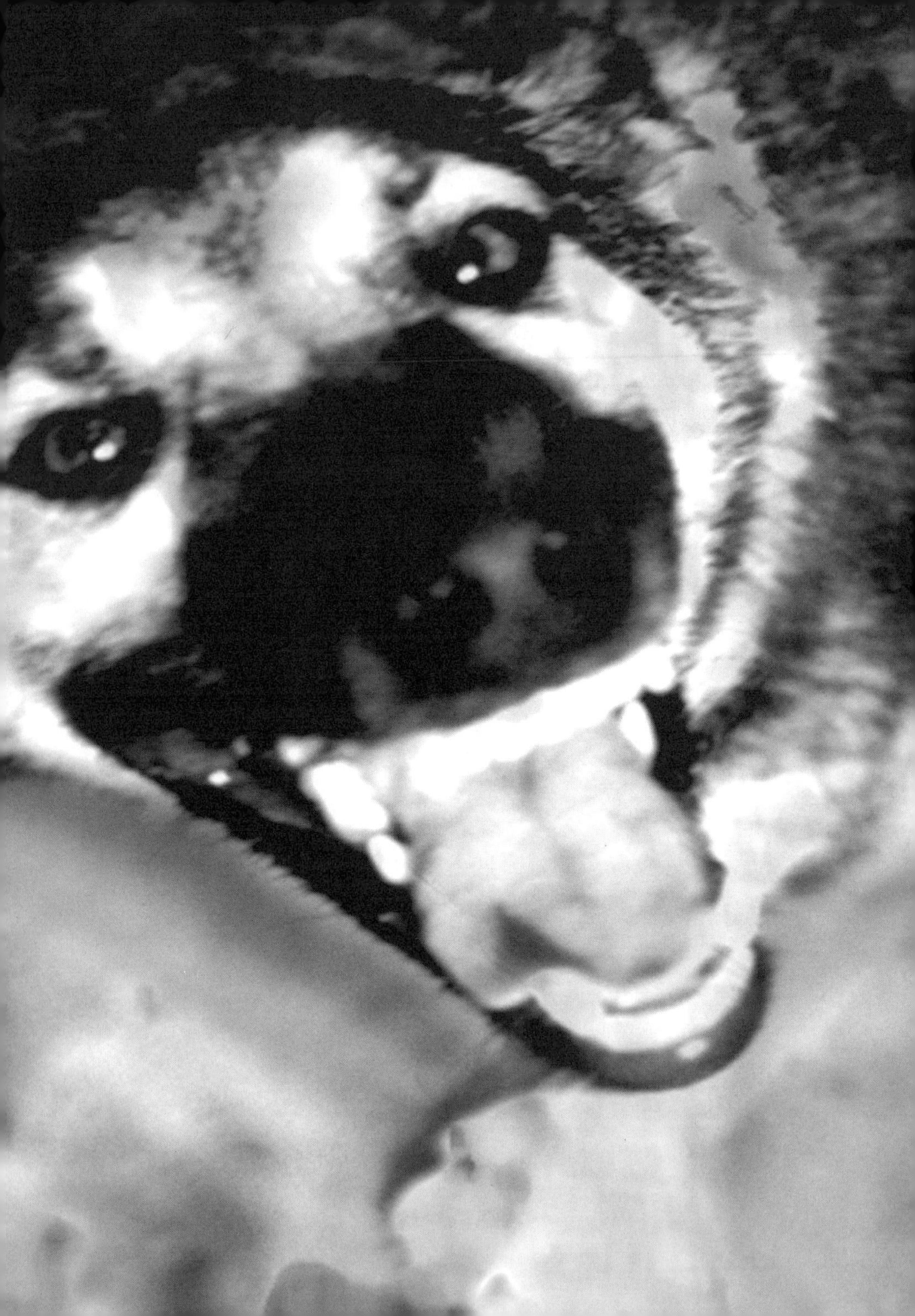

Before I answer that question, let me say that there may be such things as *vampires* and *werewolves*—at least according to Dr. David Dolphin in a report to the American Association for the Advancement of Science.[9]

The University of British Columbia biochemist studied a rare disease known as ***porphyries***, which may

CHAPTER

Are There Really Ghosts? 3

have prompted folk tales of werewolves and vampires. Porphyria victims' bodies are unable to produce heme, the red pigment in blood hemoglobin. "It is our contention that blood-drinking vampires were in fact victims of porphyria, trying to alleviate the symptoms of their dreaded disease." (Without heme, the skin becomes extremely sensitive to sunlight.) "Exposure to even mild sunlight can be devastating," according to Dolphin. Thus, all the hoaky horror flicks about creatures of the night.

But what about the transformation from mild-mannered man to hairy creature? For porphyria victims, sunlight causes skin sores that can so deform hands that they slowly begin to resemble paws. Lips and gums become taut, exposing the teeth. And to complete the werewolf look, the body tries to protect itself from light by **increased hair growth**.

Okay, Doc, but what about the stories of repelling vampires and werewolves with garlic? Dolphin's research shows that, for some reason, porphyria victims are also violently allergic to the spaghetti seasoning.

So a group of people suffering from a horrible disease turns into stories about vampires and werewolves. I believe the same thing happens with ghost stories. An unusual—but usually explainable—phenomenon gets exaggerated in the retelling.

For instance, one of the most publicized "hauntings" was the Amityville Horror. In 1974, 24-year-old Ronald DeFeo shot his parents, two brothers, and two sisters to death in their home in Amityville, Long Island, New York. During the trial, DeFeo claimed that voices in the house had been telling him to kill his family. Those are facts recorded in court documents.

One year later, the scene of the crime was purchased by George and Kathy Lutz. That, too, is a verified fact. One month later, the Lutzes suddenly moved out, claiming to be tormented by "strange voices seeming to come from within themselves." They also described "a power charge which actually lifted Mrs. Lutz off her feet toward a closet behind which was a room not noted on any blueprints."[10]

The couple hired a professional writer, Jay Anson, to ghostwrite (no pun intended) an account of their month of horror in the house. The book—which allegedly reports "the true story" of "diabolical voices, visions of the mass murderer, and everything from a plague of flies to a plague of demons"—became a best-selling book in 1977. It was transformed into a box-office success, which further exaggerated the events of the book.

Every independent investigation of the case found that the evidence for the sensational events of the book and movie depended solely on the word of the Lutzes. Even the writer, Jay Anson, admitted that he didn't know what was real or fiction—he simply wrote what the Lutzes told him. And the present owners of the famous house report no strange experiences.

Can ghosts really haunt people?

Can ghosts really make houses smell and lights go on and off?

Frank Podmore is a pioneer in psychic research. In his investigations, he discovered that firsthand accounts written by people who actually had "been there" tell of strange noises, broken objects, and relatively "unspectacular events." Several months later, however, those same people told much more "impressive" stories. And secondhand accounts—from people who had heard about the haunting but not actually witnessed it—were even more interesting.

So exaggeration in the retelling may explain some ghostly appearances. Recently, the creators of *The Blair Witch Project* movie, book, and website have convinced some people that the movie is an actual documentary and that there really was a "Blair Witch." **There wasn't!**

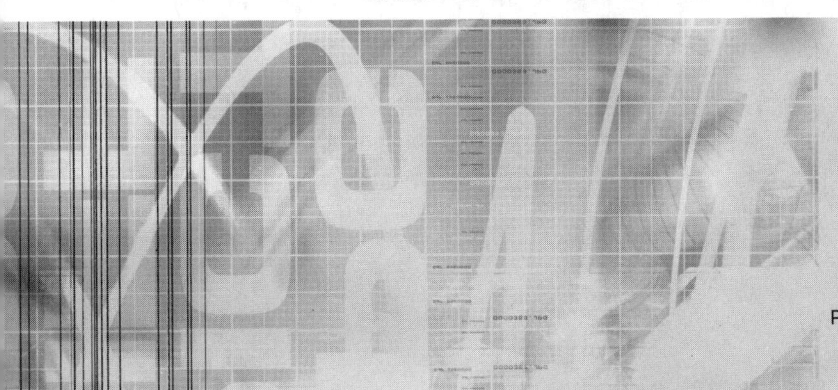

Can you come back from the dead as a ghost?

But psychiatrist and author Paul Meier has an additional explanation. He tells the story of a 5-year-old girl. As her father was being carried away to an ambulance after a heart attack, he promised, "Don't worry, dear. I'll be back." Unfortunately, the man did not survive. The girl later reported that the ghost of her father came back each night to tuck her into bed.

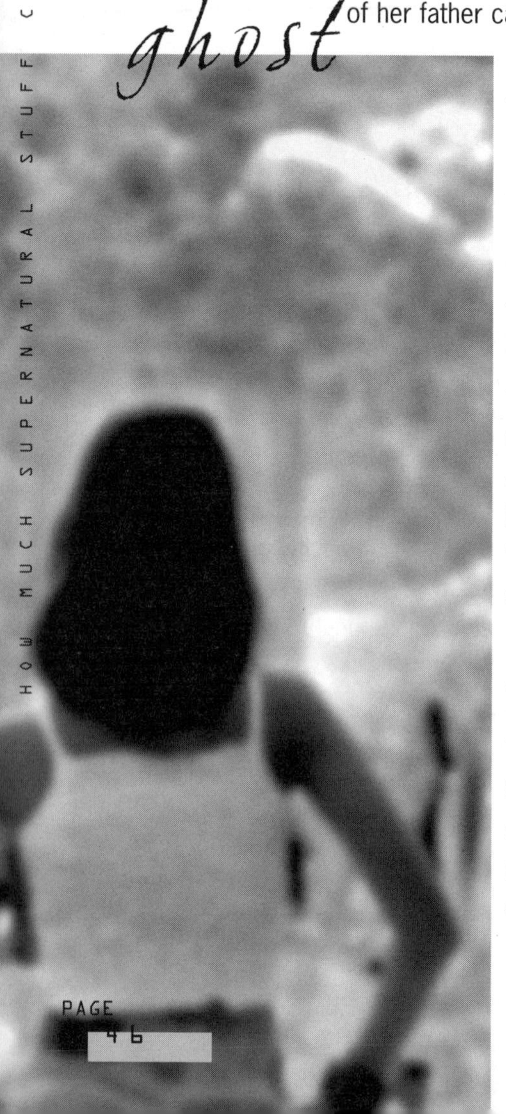

Meier claims that after the girl had intensive therapy and tranquilizers, the "ghost" disappeared. He also points out that "voices" always disappear when antipsychotic medication is prescribed. "Deceased 'spirits' must really hate that stuff!" he adds.

The psychiatrist believes that virtually all "ghosts" are auditory or visual hallucinations. "About 3 percent of the American population is psychotic or borderline psychotic at any one time. Many of these persons really believe they communicate with the dead, 'hearing' voices of deceased loved ones as clearly as if they were audible."[11]

Can you be a Christian and still believe in ghosts?

Some people claim the Bible teaches the existence of ghosts. After all, Scripture uses the word seven times! However, the word *ghost* in the King James Version is actually a mistranslation. In the Old Testament Hebrew, *nephesh* should be translated *breath*, as in "breath of life." In New Testament Greek, *pneuma* ought to be translated *breath* or *spirit*. So there isn't even a *Holy Ghost*, but a *hagios pneumos* or *Holy Spirit*. (We'll talk more about the **Holy Spirit** in chapter 13.)

How can you see ghosts?

Various "proofs" for the existence of ghosts have been offered, such as "ghost photography" (which, in virtually every case, has turned out to be film defects or deliberate double exposures) and "ghost recordings" (muffled, distorted recordings that only the person doing the recording can seem to understand). Again, every "proof" has been explained away as innocent or deliberate **fraud**.

If ghost stories are just stories, why do people make them up?

Ghost stories, then, seem to fall into **four** categories:

1. Actual, unusual events that become exaggerated in the retelling (e.g., vampires and werewolves).
2. Events that are made up for fame or financial gain (e.g., the Amityville Horror and ghost photos). For instance, one 14-year-old wrote on my survey, "My brother and my cousin said they have seen a ghost with red eyes. They seemed so serious and really think they did." It sounds like the popular slumber party stunt of making the ghost of "Mary Worth" appear in the mirror. I'd be willing to bet a bag of Oreos that these guys have become really popular around the youth camp bonfire with their "real" ghost story. Even people who "see" Elvis get national coverage.

3. Events that seem very real to the people but can be explained away by extreme grief over the deceased person or by chemical imbalances in their brains.

Are ghosts the same as demons?

4. Finally, it's possible that the phenomenon is demonic rather than ghostly. (We'll talk about demons in chapter 19.)

Or maybe it's an overwhelming desire for **immortality** (or watching Patrick Swayze and Demi Moore in *Ghost* too many times) that makes some people want to believe in ghosts. Werewolves and vampires may exist. **But ghosts? No way!**

You've probably seen infomercials for the Psychic Friends Network or scanned the horoscopes in magazines and newspapers. All promise to give us a **sneak preview** of the future: Does that cute guy in algebra class really like you? Is this a good time to make a major decision? Should I travel now? Will I finish reading this chapter?

CHAPTER

Can Pyschics Really Tell the Future?

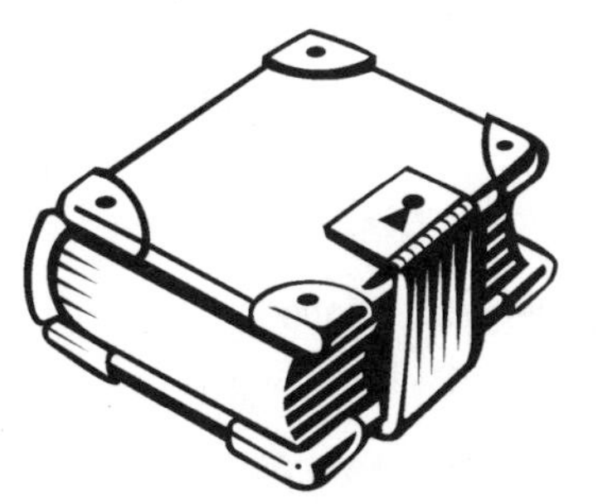

(Maybe. Could be. Perhaps. Please do!)

Astrology is based on the belief that the position of the stars, along with the phase in which you were born, determines your destiny. Astrologers give readings of the future based on the zodiac sign, which is determined by the day a person was born. Psychics can "read" the future because of the "aura" given off by the person. For instance, here are the traits of those born under each zodiac sign, followed by advice from a famous psychic. (Read your own before reading any others.)

Aries

(March 21-April 20)

Those born under this sign are imaginative and sensitive, compassionate and kind, selfless and unworldly, intuitive and sympathetic.

The stars reveal that an old friend will have the answer for an important decision you are facing. The loss of many lives will make national news during this phase, so this is a good time to re-evaluate your own relationships. Resolve a long-standing disagreement or misunderstanding with a family member. Don't be discouraged by a personal failure; success will follow during this time period.

Taurus (April 21-May 20)

Those born under this sign are adventurous and energetic, pioneering and courageous, enthusiastic and confident, dynamic and quick-witted.

The stars reveal that the loss of many lives will make national news during this phase, so this is a good time to re-evaluate your own relationships. Resolve a long-standing disagreement or misunderstanding with a family member. Don't be discouraged by a personal failure; success will follow during this time period. An old friend will have the answer for an important decision you are facing.

GEMINI (May 21-June 21)

Those born under this sign are patient and reliable, warmhearted and loving, persistent and determined, placid and security-loving.

The stars indicate it's time to resolve a long-standing disagreement or misunderstanding with a family member. Don't be discouraged by a personal failure; success will follow during this time period. An old friend will have the answer for an important decision you are facing. The loss of many lives will make national news during this phase, so this is a good time to re-evaluate your own relationships.

CANCER (June 22-July 22)

Those born under this sign are adaptable and versatile, communicative and witty, intellectual and eloquent, youthful and lively.

The stars advise, don't be discouraged by a personal failure; success will follow during this time period. An old friend will have the answer for an important decision you are facing. The loss of many lives will make national news during this phase, so this is a good time to re-evaluate your own relationships. Resolve a long-standing disagreement or misunderstanding with a family member.

LEO (July 23-August 23)

Those born under this sign are emotional and loving, intuitive and imaginative, shrewd and cautious, protective and sympathetic.

The stars reveal that an old friend will have the answer for an important decision you are facing. The loss of many lives will make national news during this phase, so this is a good time to re-evaluate your own relationships. Resolve a long-standing disagreement or misunderstanding with a family member. Don't be discouraged by a personal failure; success will follow during this time period.

VIRGO (August 24-September 22)

Those born under this sign are generous and warmhearted, creative and enthusiastic, broad-minded and expansive, faithful and loving.

The stars reveal that the loss of many lives will make national news during this phase, so this is a good time to re-evaluate your own relationships. Resolve a long-standing disagreement or misunderstanding with a family member. Don't be discouraged by a personal failure; success will follow during this time period. An old friend will have the answer for an important decision you are facing.

LIBRA (September 23-October 22)

Those born under this sign are modest and shy, meticulous and reliable, practical and diligent, intelligent and analytical.

The stars indicate that this is a good time to re-evaluate your own relationships since the loss of many lives will make national news during this phase. Resolve a long-standing disagreement or misunderstanding with a family member. Don't be discouraged by a personal failure; success will follow during this time period. An old friend will have the answer for an important decision you are facing.

SCORPIO (October 23-November 21)

Those born under this sign are diplomatic and urbane, romantic and charming, easygoing and sociable, idealistic and peaceable.

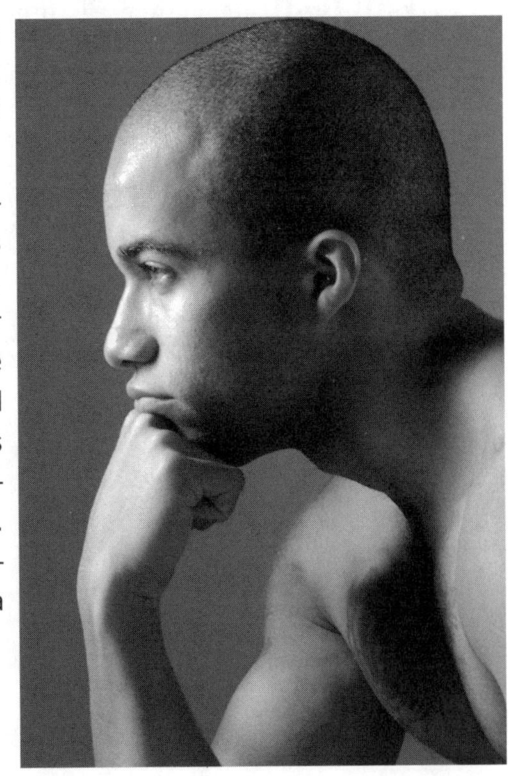

The stars advise, don't be discouraged by a personal failure; success will follow during this time period. An old friend will have the answer for an important decision you are facing. The loss of many lives will make national news during this phase, so this is a good time to re-evaluate your own relationships. Resolve a long-standing disagreement or misunderstanding with a family member.

SAGITTARIUS (November 22-December 21)

Those born under this sign are determined and forceful, emotional and intuitive, powerful and passionate, exciting and magnetic.

The stars reveal that an old friend will have the answer for an important decision you are facing. The loss of many lives will make national news during this phase, so this is a good time to re-evaluate your own relationships. Resolve a long-standing disagreement or misunderstanding with a family member. Don't be discouraged by a personal failure; success will follow during this time period.

CAPRICORN (December 22-January 19)

Those born under this sign are optimistic and freedom-loving, jovial and good-humored, honest and straightforward, intellectual and philosophical.

The stars indicate that the loss of many lives will make national news during this phase, so this is a good time to re-evaluate your own relationships. Resolve a long-standing disagreement or misunderstanding with a family member. Don't be discouraged by a personal failure; success will follow during this time period. An old friend will have the answer for an important decision you are facing.

AQUARIUS (January 20-February 18)

Those born under this sign are practical and prudent, ambitious and disciplined, patient and careful, humorous and reserved.

The stars indicate it's time to resolve a long-standing disagreement or misunderstanding with a family member. Don't be discouraged by a personal failure; success will follow during this time period. An old friend will have the answer for an important decision you are facing. The loss of many lives will make national news during this phase, so this is a good time to re-evaluate your own relationships.

PISCES (February 19-March 20)

Those born under this sign are friendly and humanitarian, honest and loyal, original and inventive, independent and intellectual.

The stars advise, don't be discouraged by a personal failure; success will follow during this time period. An old friend will have the answer for an important decision you are facing. The loss of many lives will make national news during this phase, so this is a good time to re-evaluate your own relationships. Resolve a long-standing disagreement or misunderstanding with a family member.

How can psychics know things about people that no one knows but them?

How close was our astrologer in assessing your personality traits and our psychic in predicting what issues you are dealing with? If you're like most people, you're probably thinking, "Wow, that's amazing! How did he know that?!"

Well, actually, I shifted the astrological traits up one category, so your alleged traits are actually listed in the sign below your actual sign. For instance, Aries characteristics are actually listed under Taurus; Pisces traits are listed under Aries. And the psychic advice is **identical**—except for the order—in each of the signs. Oh, one more thing: *I'm* the "psychic."

Here's my point. Astrologers and psychics are counting on the fact that you want to believe them. The characteristics of the various zodiac signs are so vague, we could talk ourselves into believing "that's me"! And astrologers and psychics are depending on you to interpret their general predictions according to your specific situation. Say, for instance, you did poorly on a test this week. If you really believe in my psychic powers, you will interpret the vague word "failure" as "C- in algebra." Wow, Swami Watkins knew that! No, I didn't. But I do know that every single one of us is going to fail at something this week.

Astrologers and psychics get into trouble when they try to predict **specific** events.

Can psychics really tell the future?

For instance, Jean Dixon, who had a best-selling book in the 1960s, gained fame for predicting the assassination of President John F. Kennedy. Then, again, so did my chronically conservative grandfather: "Somebody's gonna kill that young, liberal whippersnapper." What doesn't appear on Dixon's resume is that she also predicted that Richard Nixon would win the 1960 election—not Kennedy—and that the Russians would beat us to the moon. She had a 6 percent record for accuracy during her career!

I did much better when I wrote the "Swami Watkins" column in which I predicted my high school's sports scores. I had a 95 percent record and accurately predicted that the season's golf tournament would be rained out. My inspiration was not psychic powers but knowing a bit about the records of our various sports teams—and incredible luck.

For the last 10 years, I've tracked the New Years' predictions that the tabloids run each December or January. Here are some of the events they've predicted:

☆ In 1990, *The National Enquirer*'s panel of "10 leading psychics" predicted that "a meteorite will plow into the White House Rose Garden," "deep sea explorers will find ... artifacts from an alien spaceship," and "Soviet cosmonauts will be shocked to discover an abandoned alien space station—with the bodies of several ETs aboard." (Wrong! Unless you believe the government is covering up the alien discoveries. If so, re-read chapter 1.)

☆ The next year, *The National Enquirer* was predicting "The U.S. government will admit that aliens have contacted us after a UFO attempts to communicate with a NASA space shuttle," "Tom Cruise will lose his hair," and "Saddam Hussein will be killed in February in an accidental nuclear explosion at a secret Iraqi installation." (Wrong again!)

☆ "Vanna White will be electrocuted while turning letters on 'Wheel of Fortune' " and "Michael Jackson will lose his voice" were predicted for 1992 by *The National Enquirer*. Meanwhile, the *Sun* offered its "Bible Predictions for 1992," including the news that an "earthquake that will devour a huge portion of California" and "peace will finally come to Israel and all the nations of the Middle East in 1992—after a UFO with an alien diplomat lands near Jerusalem." (Wrong! Wrong! Wrong!)

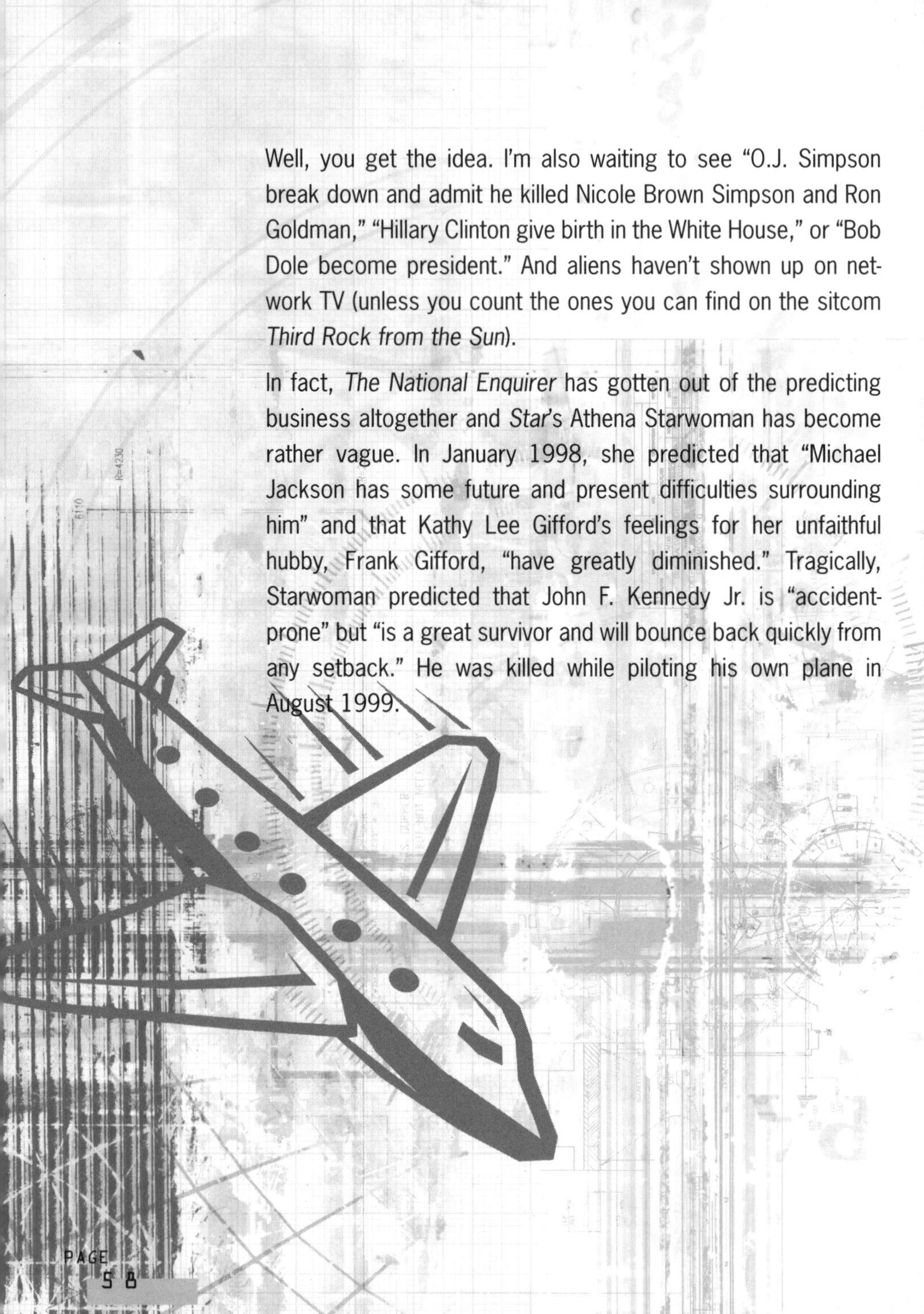

Well, you get the idea. I'm also waiting to see "O.J. Simpson break down and admit he killed Nicole Brown Simpson and Ron Goldman," "Hillary Clinton give birth in the White House," or "Bob Dole become president." And aliens haven't shown up on network TV (unless you count the ones you can find on the sitcom *Third Rock from the Sun*).

In fact, *The National Enquirer* has gotten out of the predicting business altogether and *Star*'s Athena Starwoman has become rather vague. In January 1998, she predicted that "Michael Jackson has some future and present difficulties surrounding him" and that Kathy Lee Gifford's feelings for her unfaithful hubby, Frank Gifford, "have greatly diminished." Tragically, Starwoman predicted that John F. Kennedy Jr. is "accident-prone" but "is a great survivor and will bounce back quickly from any setback." He was killed while piloting his own plane in August 1999.

Can you be a Christian and a psychic too?

For people of faith, the Bible is pretty clear on the subjects of astrology, horoscopes, and psychics, which it calls "divination" and "sorcery."

> Let no one be found among you who ... practices divination or sorcery, interprets omens, engages in witchcraft, or casts spells, or who is a medium or spiritist or who consults the dead. Anyone who does these things is detestable to the LORD, and because of these detestable practices the LORD your God will drive out those nations before you. (Deuteronomy 18:10-12)

In the New Testament, new converts to Christianity rejected their old pagan practices:

> Many of those who believed now came and openly confessed their evil deeds. A number who had practiced sorcery brought their scrolls together and burned them publicly. When they calculated the value of the scrolls, the total came to fifty thousand drachmas.[12] (Acts 19:18-19)

So should you trust the stars (or the *Star*) for your life decisions? "Swami" Watkins advises no.

What a fatal career move! Here I've been trying to make a living writing for people with a pulse when the BIG MONEY is in talking to the dead!

CHAPTER

5 Can You Talk to the Dead?

James Van Praagh, the multimillion-dollar medium, enjoyed the high life atop the *New York Times* best-seller list for weeks. His "how-to" book allegedly explains how to communicate with those who lack brain waves. The author of *Talking to Heaven* claims he is, and I quote, "a survival evidence medium." He writes that he is "able to bridge the gap between two planes of existence, that of the living and that of the dead, by providing evidential proof of life after death via detailed messages."

As a person of faith, I believe in life after death. But, I've got to admit, I don't believe in medium Van Praagh or any of his psychic friends.

How can psychics know things about people that no one knows but the person?

Here's medium Van Praagh's secret: Be vague; be very vague. On *Good Morning America*, he amazed a New York writer by telling her that her father wanted to talk about shoes. She immediately burst into tears. "I used to polish my dad's shoes." Now, the majority of people in civilized society wear **shoes**. The medium only provided a very general category, and the woman filled in the specific details herself. He then followed this lead to provide other "amazing details" such as "he likes shiny shoes."

Van Praagh explains his vagueness by the fact that he doesn't hear voices (that should reassure a court-appointed psychiatrist), but he senses the deceased person's feelings. "I sense laughter," he told another subject on the talk show *The View*. "Yes," she gushed. "My uncle had a wonderful sense of humor." Another safe guess. Everyone (except IRS auditors) has a sense of humor.

"Psychic Friends" and Van Praagh depend on their subjects' deep desire to believe in their powers. That's why psychics begin with vague statements, such as, "Is there a conflict in your life?" Well, duh, who doesn't have conflict! Next question, "Does it involve someone close to you?" Duh, again. The subject—who's often paying $3.95 a minute in phone charges or $250 per session with Van Praagh—provides all the answers for the clever psychic! ("I see you losing a great deal of money!")

If these **frauds** really had psychic powers, they wouldn't have to play investigative reporter. And Van Praagh seemed to be wrong as many times as he was right. He had a message from beyond from a *living* person on the morning news show. (The ancient Hebrews ensured the survival of the fittest prophets by killing those who didn't have *perfect* prediction records.)

Van Praagh's success is based on our deep desire to know something about life after death. That's perfectly normal and understandable. But save your 20 bucks—don't bother to buy his book. The Gideons will *give* you a Bible, which provides much more specifics on life after death, absolutely free. (We talked about the afterlife in book two of this series—and it's a lot cheaper than Van Praagh's book!)

Can you be a psychic and a Christian?

Under the Old Testament law, claiming to contact the dead was **punishable** with one's own death (Exodus 22:18; Deuteronomy 18:9–14). So why is there a story of the king of Israel talking to a dead prophet in the Bible?!

King Saul, who had lost favor with God, was desperate for advice on how to defeat the Philistines. (They were still pretty steamed after David killed their local folk hero, Goliath).

> Saul then said to his attendants, "Find me a woman who is a medium, so I may go and inquire of her."
>
> "There is one in Endor," they said.
>
> So Saul disguised himself, putting on other clothes, and at night he and two men went to the woman. "Consult a spirit for me," he said, "and bring up for me the one I name."
>
> But the woman said to him, "Surely you know

what Saul has done. He has cut off the mediums and spiritists from the land. Why have you set a trap for my life to bring about my death?"

Saul swore to her by the LORD, "As surely as the LORD lives, you will not be punished for this."

Then the woman asked, "Whom shall I bring up for you?"

"Bring up Samuel," he said.

When the woman saw Samuel, she cried out at the top of her voice and said to Saul, "Why have you deceived me? You are Saul!"

The king said to her, "Don't be afraid. What do you see?"

The woman said, "I see a spirit coming up out of the ground."

"What does he look like?" he asked.

"An old man wearing a robe is coming up," she said.

Then Saul knew it was Samuel, and he bowed down and prostrated himself with his face to the ground.

Samuel said to Saul, "Why have you disturbed me by bringing me up?"

"I am in great distress," Saul said. "The Philistines are fighting against me, and God has turned away from me. He no longer answers me, either by prophets or by dreams. So I have called on you to tell me what to do."

Samuel said, "Why do you consult me, now that the LORD has turned away from you and become your enemy? The LORD has done what He predicted through me. The LORD has torn the kingdom out of your hands and given it to one of your neighbors—to David. Because you did not obey the LORD or carry out His fierce wrath against the Amalekites, the LORD has done this to you today. The LORD will hand over both Israel and you to the Philistines, and tomorrow you and your sons will be with me. The LORD will also hand over the army of Israel to the Philistines." (1 Samuel 28:7-19)

So was this **authentic** communication with the dead? Bible commentator Adam Clark believes that it was an "angel of God" who brought the prophecy of Saul's own death. Another Bible scholar, Matthew Henry, believes it was a satanic manifestation.

But psychic investigator and stage magician Danny Korem has the most interesting theory. In the original Hebrew of the Old Testament, the word *both* is translated as *medium*. Some versions translate the word as *one with a familiar spirit*, but at the time this book of the Bible was written, the word also meant *ventriloquist*.

Korem speculates that the "witch of Endor" was nothing more than a clever voice-thrower and that Saul was the real dummy. Remember, Saul never sees "Samuel." The medium describes what she sees as "an old man wrapped in a robe." That would have described any male over 50! And Korem believes that her prediction is simply a calculated guess or "self-fulfilling prophecy." Whatever the explanation, there isn't sufficient proof to claim that Samuel really did come back from the dead.

Those who are determined to prove that the Bible teaches communication with the dead also turn to the New Testament.

"There was a rich man who was dressed in purple and fine linen and lived in luxury every day. At his gate was laid a beggar named Lazarus, covered with sores and longing to eat what fell from the rich man's table. Even the dogs came and licked his sores.

The time came when the beggar died and the angels carried him to Abraham's side. The rich man also died and was buried. In hell, where he was in torment, he looked up and saw Abraham far away, with Lazarus by his side. So he called to him, 'Father Abraham, have pity on me and send Lazarus to dip the tip of his finger in water and cool my tongue, because I am in agony in this fire.'

But Abraham replied, 'Son, remember that in your lifetime you received your good things, while Lazarus received bad things, but now he is comforted here and you are in agony. And besides all this, between us and you a great chasm has been fixed, so that those who want to go from here to you cannot, nor can anyone cross over from there to us.'

He answered, 'Then I beg you, father, send Lazarus to my father's house, for I have five brothers. Let him warn them, so that they will not also come to this place of torment.'

Abraham replied, 'They have Moses and the Prophets; let them listen to them.'

'No, father Abraham,' he said, 'but if someone from the dead goes to them, they will repent.' He said to him, 'If they do not listen to Moses and the Prophets, they will not be convinced even if someone rises from the dead.'" (Luke 16:19-31)

First, Jesus has been speaking in parables, which are earthly stories that reveal an eternal truth. So Jesus may not be relating an actual event. If we were to take all parables literally, we would all be wearing wool ("The Lost Sheep") with "In God We Trust" stamped on our back sides ("The Lost Coin") while living in a pigpen ("The Prodigal Son"). And most commentators also believe that Jesus is referring to His own resurrection as He concludes the parable, not an appearance by Lazarus.

Second, the parable seems to imply that communication from the dead to the living is improbable if not impossible. But the living seem to have an unstoppable desire to believe it is possible.

During the middle 1800s, "spiritism" became popularized by the famous Fox sisters of Rochester, New York. These women claimed that a murdered peddler was communicating with them by "rapping." (*Rapping* at that time meant tapping sounds, not to be confused with the modern musical style). Their nationwide fame turned out to be a "bum rap" when one of the psychic sisters confessed that she made the sounds by deliberately cracking her knee joints.

Harry **Houdini**, the famous escape artist, became interested in spiritism while trying to contact his mother. He continued his study of psychic phenomenon after reading *Revelations of a Spirit Medium*. The unnamed author revealed how he became interested in spiritism and tried to develop his own psychic powers, only to discover it was all a fake. The book revealed how mediums could slip in and out of knotted ropes and escape from "spirit cabinets" to create their "spirit manifestations."

Thus, Houdini's career turned to tricky escapes. He also duplicated any effect that any medium allegedly accomplished through spirits. In each town, he would challenge local psychics to perform their "manifestations" on stage. Then Houdini would duplicate them through completely natural means.

Scientific American used Houdini as a judge in a $5,000 challenge. The magazine promised to give half the money to the first medium who could prove a case of spirit phenomenon, such as table tipping or "spirit writing." The second half would go to any medium who could prove communication with the dead. No one claimed the prize money.

Houdini continued to search for authentic communication and manifestations from the dead, but never found any. He also promised to send a message back from the other side, if at all possible. Bess Houdini offered **$10,000** to any medium who could reveal a 10-word message her husband had promised to send back from the dead. So on each anniversary of the master magician's death on Halloween night, séances have been held to receive a message from Harry Houdini. He has never phoned home.

More recently, professional magician and skeptic James "The Amazing" Randi began offering $10,000 to anyone who could perform a genuine psychic or paranormal act under controlled conditions. In 1997, he raised the stakes to $1,000,000. After hundreds of applicants and dozens of tested subjects, Randi still has his money.

Can you contact the dead through séances?

Ouija boards have become a popular method of communicating with the dead and peeking into the future—especially at junior high sleepovers. A triangular pointer called a *planchette* supposedly glides across a board printed with an alphabet, "Yes," "No," and "Good-bye." But what **force** guides the planchette to spell out messages from "beyond"?

Isaac Fuld, who created and patented the "game," admitted the mobilizing force was simply "involuntary muscle actions," though he did suggest the possibility that "some other agency" spelled out the messages. Obviously a shrewd marketing ploy![13]

Paul Meier, a Christian psychiatrist, believes that any results obtained from Ouija boards are by "trickery, luck, or subconscious ideomotor action."[14] Danny Korem, the psychic investigator, also claims that he has not uncovered one Ouija board story that can't be explained with subconscious movement of the planchette.

I agree that most psychic phenomenon is strictly sophisticated fakery. But the Bible provides a second possible explanation.

> Once when we were going to the place of prayer, we were met by a slave girl who had a spirit by which she predicted the future. She earned a great deal of money for her owners by fortune-telling. This girl followed Paul and the rest of us, shouting, "These men are servants of the Most High God, who are telling you the way to be saved." She kept this up for many days.

> Finally Paul became so troubled that he turned around and said to the spirit, "In the name of Jesus Christ I command you to come out of her!" At that moment the spirit left her. When the owners of the slave girl realized that their hope of making money was gone, they seized Paul and Silas and dragged them into the marketplace to face the authorities. (Acts 16:16-19)

It's possible that "psychic" phenomenon can be accomplished by satanic powers, which is a great reason to stay away from it all. But keep in mind that Satan doesn't have to spend a lot of time here because "psychics" can fool most of the people most of the time all by themselves.

Jana sat across from me in the youth camp dining hall after all the other teens had left.

"I've got a question for you," she began.

"Okay," I said.

"What if all these Christian teachings aren't true? I've got an aunt who's really into the **New Age**—

CHAPTER

6 Is the Bible Really True?

you know, crystals and channeling—and she really believes in it. I mean, she believes in it more than I believe in Christianity."

"Well, it really doesn't matter *that* you believe," I responded.

Jana stared at me as if she was going into shock. I hurried to explain. "Say, for instance, you believed—absolutely, wholeheartedly, sincerely—that this **saltshaker** was your ticket to heaven." She continued to stare at me without saying a word. "Would believing it make it true?" I asked.

"No," she finally answered.

"So it's not *that* you believe but *what* you believe or, in this case, in *whom* you believe."

"Okay, I can see that. But how can you know that the Bible and Jesus and Christianity are the right things to believe and everything else is wrong? Aren't there a lot of ways to heaven?"

Aren't there a lot of ways to heaven?

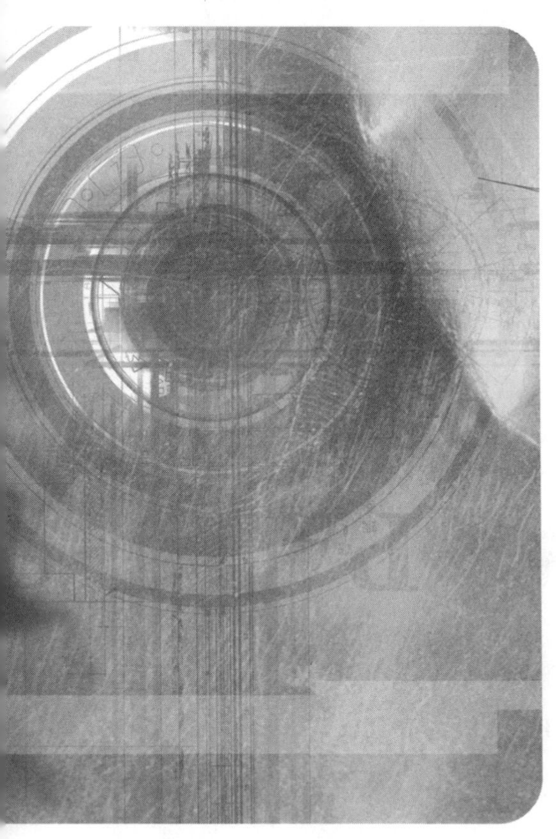

I continued, "Jesus doesn't allow any alternate routes to heaven. He declared, 'I am the way and the truth and the life. No one comes to the Father except through Me'" (John 14:6).

"Okay, but how can I know that what Jesus said was true?" she continued.

"By asking the same tough questions we asked about reincarnation in yesterday's seminar," I answered. (We cover this in book two of *The Why Files.*) And with that we were off on a good discussion about the same questions raised throughout this book:

1. Are the 66 books of the Bible credible? Can we believe what they say?
2. Can we confirm the truth of the Bible's stories about God and the world? Are there reliable eyewitnesses to the events recorded in the Bible?

3. Are the books of the Bible consistent with one another?
4. Do the Bible's history and observations agree with other historical and scientific evidence?

If you, like Jana, are seriously questioning whether biblical teachings about angels, demons, and God are accurate, it will be worth your time to consider the following evidence.

Isn't the Bible unscientific?

Keep in mind that simply because something is hard to believe doesn't make it false. And just because something can't be "scientifically proven" doesn't make it untrue. Remember in the introduction we discussed how you couldn't prove "scientifically" that you sank an "unbelievable" basket from half court. Such scientific evidence would demand that you readily repeat the feat in a controlled setting. But we can prove that you made the basket with "historical proof"—which *isn't* scientific proof! Written reports of **eyewitnesses** are the only way we know that Julius Caesar ruled the Roman Empire, that the Pilgrims landed at Plymouth Rock, or that President Abraham Lincoln was assassinated.

Let's look at our questions one at a time.

1. **Are the 66 books of the Bible credible? Can we believe what they say?**

Although numerous writers contributed books to what we now know as the Bible, they all wrote by the **inspiration** of a single source—God. In various places in His Word, God tells us that the human writers weren't working on their own. Paul writes that "all Scripture is God-breathed" (2 Timothy 3:16) and Peter writes that "prophecy never had its origin in the will of man, but men spoke from God as they were carried along by the Holy Spirit" 2 Peter 1:21). And we know we can believe what these men wrote because God does not lie (Numbers 23:19; Titus 1:2).

Now that we've established the truthfulness of the books and their writers, let's look at what these books say about Jesus Christ. We start here because

all Scripture points to Jesus Christ

and the salvation we have through Him.

Let's start with the most difficult question: Is Jesus really the Son of God, or is He, as many would argue, simply a very good man? Jesus Himself claimed to be God (Mark 9:37; John 12:44; 14:9). He accepted worship (Matthew 14:33; Luke 5:8; John 20:28). He told His followers to pray in His name (John 16:23). He even forgave people's sins (Matthew 9:2–7; Mark 2:5–7; Luke 7:47–48). Only God could do these things.

C. S. Lewis claimed that Jesus couldn't be a "good man." He was either Lord, a liar, or a lunatic.

> I am trying here to prevent anyone saying the really foolish thing that people often say about Him: "I'm ready to accept Jesus as a great moral teacher, but I don't accept His claim to be God." That is the one thing we must not say. A man who was merely a man and said the sort of things Jesus said would not be a great moral teacher. He would either be a lunatic—on the level with the man who says he is a poached egg—or else he would be the Devil of Hell. You must make your choice. Either this man was, and is, the Son of God: or else a madman or something worse. You can shut Him up for a fool, you can spit at Him and kill Him as a demon; or you can fall at His feet and call Him Lord and God. But let us not come with any patronizing nonsense about His being a great human teacher. He has not left that open to us. He did not intend to.[15]

Some argue, however, that Christ never claimed to be Lord. Instead, later editors slipped these "divine" delusions into the biblical manuscripts. But as we'll discuss later, there are **24,000** ancient New Testament manuscripts available for scrutiny, so any later attempt at deception would surely be exposed. It hasn't been! The biblical statements that Jesus is God are true. And if these are true, then we also can believe Jesus' statement that He is the only way to heaven.

How do we know the Bible is true?

Again, we know the Bible is true because we believe God when He calls it His Word; God does not lie. But you also can make the argument that the Bible is true because the Old Testament prophecies of the Messiah are fulfilled in Jesus Christ. God revealed to the godly men who recorded the Old Testament books events that would occur hundreds and even thousands of years in the **future**. Centuries before His birth, the ancient prophets made amazing God-directed predictions that were accurately and precisely fulfilled in Jesus Christ.

But couldn't first-century editors have slipped these prophecies into the writings of the B.C. writers to make it look like Christ fulfilled prophecy? If they did, they surely would have been exposed when recent archaeological digs discovered copies of these precise prophecies of Isaiah dating back to 125 B.C. (That's 125 years before Christ was born!) Unless those first-century editors had a flux-capacitor-powered chariot (ala *Back to the Future*'s **time machine**), that would have been impossible!

Aren't there a lot of contradictions in the Bible?

Let's look at some of the prophecies about the Messiah. Micah (5:2) claimed the Christ would be born in Bethlehem; Hosea (11:1) prophesied He would come out of Egypt; and another claimed He would live in Nazareth. "See," the ancient skeptics probably laughed, "Scripture contradicts itself!"

But Jesus was born in Bethlehem, hidden in Egypt to avoid the wrath of King Herod, and, once the threat was over, taken to Nazareth where He grew up (Matthew 2).

The prophet Isaiah spoke of the **miracles** Jesus would perform: "Then will the eyes of the blind be opened and the ears of the deaf unstopped. Then will the lame leap like a deer, and the mute tongue shout for joy" (Isaiah 35:5–6a). And we read of the fulfillment of this prophecy throughout the four Gospels. And many of Jesus' miracles are recorded in multiple Gospels. No mere human can do the things that history records Jesus doing!

As Christ entered Jerusalem in preparation for His death, the prophecy of Zechariah was fulfilled: "Rejoice greatly, O Daughter of Zion! Shout, Daughter of Jerusalem! See, your king comes to you, righteous and having salvation, gentle and riding on a donkey, on a colt, the foal of a donkey" (9:9). Okay, Jesus could have read this particular prophecy and deliberately planned to "fulfill" it. But He couldn't have controlled the spontaneous outpouring of praise from children in the temple that had been foretold in the book of Psalms (8:2).

Even Christ's betrayal—which would have been hard to manipulate deliberately—was foretold by the prophets in exact detail, right down to the exact amount of money given to the betrayer! The prophet Zechariah wrote that 30 pieces of silver would be the price. And he prophesied that the betrayer would return the money.

Zechariah even foretold that the betrayer would throw the money on the temple floor and that the 30 pieces would buy a potter's field (11:12–13). Again, remember that these **predictions** were in print hundreds of years before Christ was born!

Jesus' crucifixion—which no one would want to stage—also was foretold in graphic detail. The prophet Isaiah spoke of Jesus being beaten, whipped, spat upon, and crucified with thieves (50:6; 53:5, 12). The psalmist wrote of His clothing being gambled over and of His being given vinegar to drink (Psalm 22:15; 69:21). The prophet Amos foretold the darkness that covered the land during the crucifixion (8:9). The psalmist even prophesied Christ's exact words from the cross: "My God, My God, why have You forsaken Me?" (Psalm 22:1).

So maybe these were just **incredible coincidences**. Peter Stoner has estimated that the odds against one man fulfilling just eight of these prophecies is 1 in 100,000,000,000,000,000![16] Stoner helps us visualize 10^{17} (the scientific notation of 10 followed by 17 zeros). Imagine the state of Texas two feet deep in silver dollars. The odds of a blindfolded man finding a specially marked coin on the first try is 1 in 10^{17}.

And those odds are for accurately fulfilling just eight of the numerous prophecies that Christ fulfilled!

2. **Can we confirm the truth of the Bible's stories about God and the world? Are there reliable eyewitnesses to the events recorded in the Bible?**

Let's take the most outrageous, unbelievable claim in Scripture: that Jesus Christ was killed, buried, and yet rose to life again on the third day. Is it an historical act? Here's what the Bible says:

> After the Sabbath, at dawn on the first day of the week, Mary Magdalene and the other Mary went to look at the tomb.
>
> There was a violent earthquake, for an angel of the Lord came down from heaven and, going to the tomb, rolled back the stone and sat on it. His appearance was like lightning, and his clothes were white as snow. The guards were so afraid of him that they shook and became like dead men.
>
> The angel said to the women, "Do not be afraid, for I know that you are looking for Jesus, who was crucified. He is not here; He has risen, just as He said. Come and see the place where He lay. Then go quickly and tell His disciples: 'He has risen from the dead and is going ahead of you into Galilee. There you will see Him.' Now I have told you."
>
> So the women hurried away from the tomb, afraid yet filled with joy, and ran to tell His disciples. Suddenly Jesus met them. "Greetings," He said. They came to Him, clasped His feet and worshiped Him. (Matthew 28:1-9)

Wilbur Smith says: "The meaning of the resurrection is a theological matter, but the fact of the resurrection is a historical matter; the nature of the resurrection body of Jesus may be a mystery, but the fact the body disappeared from the tomb is a matter to be decided upon by historical evidence."[17]

Those who wish to explain away the resurrection run into an entire road map of **dead ends**. Some claim that Christ merely "swooned" on the cross and revived in the tomb. How can they explain that the Roman crucifixion squad, whose sole duty was to kill criminals, declared Jesus dead? Certainly these men who were experienced with executions wouldn't make such a serious mistake. How can those who say Jesus didn't die explain that a man bleeding from wounds to His head, back, wrist, and feet—along with a spear puncture in His side—could possibly revive enough to escape from mummy-like burial cloths, push away a huge boulder that sealed the tomb, and sneak past armed guards? That requires more faith to believe than that He rose from the dead!

Others claim that the disciples stole Christ's body and made up the story of the resurrection. Scripture records that

> While the women were on their way, some of the guards went into the city and reported to the chief priests everything that had happened. When the chief priests had met with the elders and devised a plan, they gave the soldiers a large sum of money, telling them, "You are to say, 'His disciples came during the night and stole Him away while we were asleep.' If this report gets to the governor, we will satisfy him and keep you out of trouble." So the soldiers took the money and did as they were instructed. And this story has been widely circulated among the Jews to this very day. (Matthew 28:11-15)

Again, the theory that Christ's disciples stole His body requires a flying leap of logic. How could the disciples, who ran into hiding after their leader's arrest, suddenly be courageous enough to fight their way through armed guards to steal Christ's body? (Only one of the apostles, John, and a few female followers had courage enough to show up at Christ's execution.) And how do we explain the fact that these selfish, cowardly disciples could go to their deaths singing and praising their resurrected Savior if it was indeed a total hoax?

Others have tried to explain Christ's resurrection by saying that His post-resurrection appearances were merely hallucinations. However, a group of **500** people saw Jesus after His resurrection (1 Corinthians 15:3–8).

Amazingly, not one record has been found in ancient writing that rejects the idea of Christ's resurrection. If it was a hoax, the residents of Jerusalem could easily have verified it as false.

3. Are the books of the Bible consistent with one another?

The Bible was written over a 1,600-year period by at least 40 different writers on three different continents in three different languages (Hebrew, Aramaic, and Greek). It covers hundreds of controversial subjects. Yet there is harmony in the text.

Yes, there are some minor details that seem to contradict one another. For instance, in the account of Jesus cursing a fruitless fig tree, Matthew records it died and withered up immediately (21:19), but Mark reports that the disciples *saw* the withered fig tree the next morning (11:20–21). There are several other seeming discrepancies in the Gospel accounts of Christ's last week on earth. Even these apparent discrepancies may have a human explanation: Eyewitnesses to the same accident will often differ on small points because of where they were in relation to the accident at the time it occurred. These "discrepancies" do not alter the fact the accident happened.

4. Do the Bible's history and observations agree with other historical and scientific evidence?

Francis Schaeffer, a Christian philosopher and former skeptic, writes:

> **Christianity involves history.** To say only that is already to have said something remarkable, because it separates the Judeo-Christian world view from almost all other religious thought. It is rooted in history. Is the history accurate?
>
> The more we understand about the Middle East between 2500 B.C. and A.D. 100, the more confident we can be that the information in **the Bible is reliable**, even when it speaks about the simple things of time and space.[18]

Josh McDowell has spent years documenting the **accuracy** of Scripture with historical and archaeological evidence. He points out that "Christianity appeals to the facts of history ... the most patent and accessible data. Christ is a fact of history as real as any other."[19]

The apostle Luke points out the historical accuracy of his gospel with these words:

> Many have undertaken to draw up an account of the things that have been fulfilled among us, just as they were handed down to us by those who from the first were eyewitnesses and servants of the word. Therefore, since I myself have carefully investigated everything from the beginning, it seemed good also to me to write an orderly account for you, most excellent Theophilus, so that you may know the certainty of the things you have been taught. (Luke 1:1-4)

Luke, who was highly educated as a medical doctor, claims to have "carefully investigated everything from the beginning." Because the Bible is credible, it stands up to historical investigation.

Aren't there a lot of errors in the Bible? Why should I believe it?

Some scholars scoffed at the idea of Moses writing the first five books of the Old Testament. They claimed that there was no written language at the time. If this argument were true, it would certainly undermine the truthfulness of the Bible! But in 1974, Paolo Matthiae discovered tablets in the region of northeast Syria that predate Moses by 1,000 years. The writings at Ebla also confirmed the existence of **biblical cities** that modern historians had claimed were simply mythical. According to these ancient tablets, Sodom and Gomorrah, as well as other "lost" cities, really did exist!

Some dismiss the Old and New Testaments because the "original manuscripts" have long since disappeared; all we have now are handmade copies. Before 1947, the oldest manuscripts of the Hebrew Old Testament written in Hebrew were dated to around A.D. 900, thousands of years after they were originally penned. So there would be plenty of time for mistakes to be made in copying the scrolls. (Remember this was hundreds of years before the printing press and the photocopy machine.)

But with the discovery of the **Dead Sea Scrolls**, manuscripts of the book of Isaiah were found that had been copied around 125 B.C.—1,000 years earlier than the previously known manuscripts. Most important, the A.D. 900 manuscripts were found to be virtual photocopies of the 125 B.C. manuscripts! So the Old Testament was transmitted accurately down through the years.

It's much better news on the New Testament front—currently 24,000 copies of the ancient texts are in existence. Sir Frederick Kenyon of the British Museum claims that the time between the original writings and the earliest dated manuscripts of New Testament books is "so small as to be in fact negligible."[20]

Compare that with other ancient literature. There are only 10 copies of the writings of the Caesar who ruled from 100–44 B.C., and those are dated 1,000 years after the originals were written. There are only seven complete manuscripts of Plato's writing (427–347 B.C.), but these date from 1,200 years after the original writing. Aristotle (384–322 B.C.) is only known from five manuscripts, all of which are dated 1,400 years after he penned his works.

From this evidence, we know the Bible has been **reproduced more accurately** than the works of ancient historians and thinkers.

Dr. Robert Wilson has been called "the outstanding authority on ancient languages of the Middle East." While investigating the Bible's record of kings who ruled the area, he found only "two or three" misspellings among the 29 kings' names listed in the Bible when compared to unearthed monuments that listed their names.

Compare that with a list of Egyptian kings uncovered at an archaeological dig of a Greek library thought to have been used in 200 B.C. Of the 38 Egyptian kings listed, only three or four of them could be verified by other archaeological evidence. The famous second-century historian Ptolemy drew up a list of the 18 kings of Babylon. Not one of them is spelled correctly when compared to ancient Babylonian monuments.

Wilson claimed, "If anyone talks against the Bible, ask him about the kings mentioned in it. There are 29 kings of Egypt, Israel, Moab, Damascus, Tyre, Babylon, Assyria, and Persia referred to and 10 different countries among these 29; all of which are included in the Bible accounts and on ancient monu-

ments. Every one of these is given his right name in the Bible, his right country, and placed in the correct chronological order."[21]

The Bible continues to stand up to historical and archaeological testing. For instance, many secular historians have dismissed Luke's account of the birth of Christ.

> In those days Caesar Augustus issued a decree that a census should be taken of the entire Roman world. (This was the first census that took place while Quirinius was governor of Syria.) And everyone went to his own town to register. (Luke 2:1-3)

Skeptics claimed there was no census during that time, that Quirinius was not the governor of Syria, and that no one had to return to his ancestors' home to register. If these charges are true, then the Bible can't be true!

But archaeologists have discovered that Caesar Augustus did indeed demand a census every 14 years—one of which occurred around 9–8 B.C. (Because of a mistake in ancient calendars, Jesus was probably born several years before A.D. 1. Ancient writings found in Antioch verify that Quirinius was governor of Syria around 7–6 B.C. And finally, an ancient inscription declares, "Because of the approaching census it is necessary that all those residing for any cause away from their homes should at once prepare to return to their own governments in order that they may complete the family registration of enrollment."[22]

It's no surprise that the Bible is right! Remember, Dr. Luke had "carefully investigated everything from the beginning."

Does the Bible **pass** the four tests we proposed? It is extremely accurate when recording history. And its prophecies relating to the birth, death, and resurrection of Christ are exceptionally accurate. So because the Bible is true in what it says about history and physical events, we also can trust what the Bible says about salvation, the future, and the supernatural as well. Actually, there's more evidence that Jesus Christ rose from the dead than that Julius Caesar ruled Rome.

"Hmmm," Jana finally said after an hour of give and take. "You've given me a lot to think about."

"That's all I'm asking you to do—consider the evidence for Christianity," I replied.

"I'll do that."

I hope you will too.

Part TWO

Is There Really a God and Angels and Everything?

What is God like?

- ? A human being with a heart, feet, eyes like fire, and He shampoos His hair every day.
- ? He has white hair and His eyes are bloodshot.
- ? Tall, black hair, wears sharp clothes and a heart necklace.

CHAPTER 7

Aren't There a Lot of Ideas about God?

- ? He looks like Billy Graham.
- ? He looks like Jesus, but I'll tell you a secret. I'm not sure, 'cause I've never seen Him.
- ? He's an old man because of all the years He's been alive.
- ? I think He's an old man with a long, gray beard. And He sits on a throne like a king of all mankind, and drinks all the Dr. Pepper He wants.

Those are some of the answers Walter Wagner received when he surveyed a children's Sunday school class in Compton, California.[23]

My survey of junior and senior high students found that young people have many more questions than answers at this stage of life. H. Orton Wiley writes, "It is not the existence of God that is in dispute, but His nature; it is not whether God is, but what He is."[24]

Here's an overview of different ideas of "what He is."

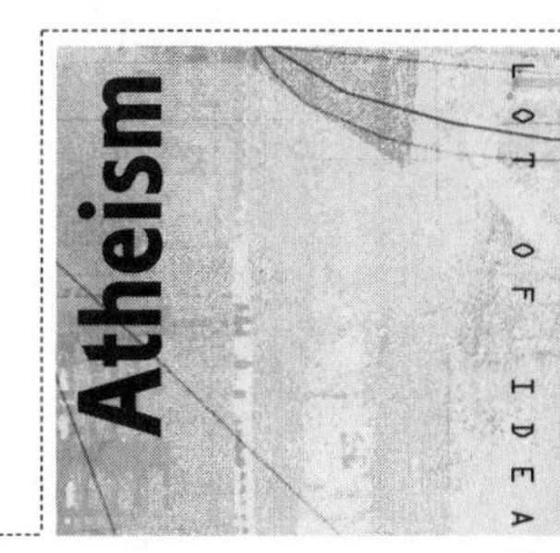

Only about 5 percent of Americans believe there is no God. Even some atheists believe that He once existed but died in the body of Jesus Christ. Other atheists believe it's impossible to know God, so He's irrelevant to "real" life. Most atheists, however, believe that God never was and the idea of God is simply a **myth**.

Many of the founders of the United States—"one nation under God"—were deists. They believed God created the universe and got it running, but they also believed He didn't act in the world He had created. Deists believe God is **beyond** the world—impersonal, all-good, all-loving, all-powerful, and all-knowing.

Deists pray to God. However, they don't believe that God ever did—or ever will—act in the lives of humans, for example, by performing miracles. And there's definitely no way Christ rose from the dead. Some of this philosophy's followers included Thomas Paine, Benjamin Franklin, and Thomas Jefferson. Jefferson removed all the miracles from his version of the Bible and left Christ in the tomb. Paine wrote that Christianity is "too absurd for belief."

Deists have no explanation of how God can create a universe from nothing but can't do anything else considered "miraculous."

Pantheism

Pantheists, such as those who follow Hinduism, Taoism, and some forms of Buddhism, believe that all is god and god is all. Broccoli, blue whales, boulders, and even our own bodies are god. New Age beliefs and modern witchcraft, as well as Christian Science, Unity, Scientology, and Theosophy, are considered pantheistic religions.

The goal of pantheists is to realize that they are god and god is everything. (We'll talk more about this in the next chapter.)

Polytheism

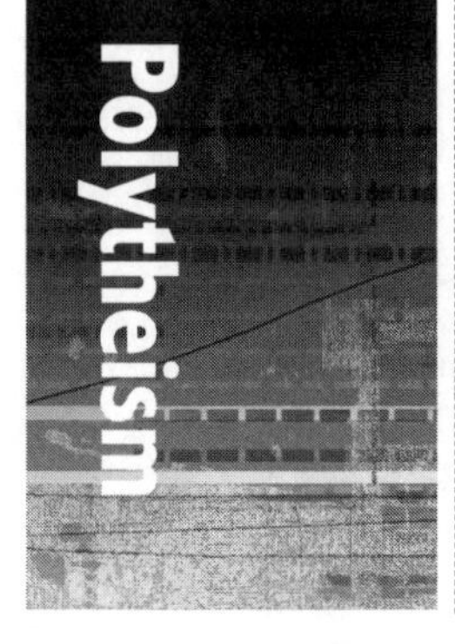

Greek, Norse, and Roman mythology are filled with many gods who rule over different realms. For instance, farming and hunting were supervised by Artemis (Greek), Freyer (Norse), or Diana (Roman).

There was a lot of sleeping around in polytheistic paradise, so the Father God (Zeus, Odin, Jupiter, respectively) and Mother God (Hera, Frigga, Juno), as well as the lesser gods, were often having children with spouses of the other gods and with unsuspecting humans.

Mormonism, which is one of the fastest growing religions in the western world, teaches that we are all gods in the making ("spirit children of the Father"). In the afterlife, Mormon wives will be continually pregnant, birthing more gods to fill their very own planet. (We'll talk more about Mormonism in chapter 21.)

Hindus are not only pantheistic, but polytheistic. They teach that a person is reincarnated to higher and higher life-forms if she improves in words, deeds, and actions. (We've devoted a whole chapter to reincarnation in the second book in this series.) In a future life, Hindus hope to reach *liberation* (*moksha*), where they expand their being and consciousness to an infinite level and realize they are god. This occurs through diligent study of the ancient writings, devotion to one of the many Hindu deities, sacrifices, ceremonies, fasting, and pilgrimages.

Monotheism

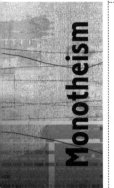

There are several religious traditions that worship only one god. Although there are different sects within **Buddhism**, those who practice the religion follow the teachings of Gautama, who lived as early as the sixth-century B.C. Buddha's last words were "... work out your salvation with diligence." His followers must do this through right knowledge, right intentions, right speech, right conduct, the right occupation, right effort, right "mindfulness," and right meditation.

The Jewish, Christian, and Islamic faiths also believe there is only one God. Although some theologians point out that all three traditions worship the same "God," each tradition has distinctly different views of the diety.

The Jewish religion teaches that God expects complete obedience of His Law as the only way to salvation. Most Jews still live in anticipation of the fulfillment of the biblical promises of the Messiah (the Son of God) found in the Old Testament, thus they deny that Jesus Christ was the promised Son of God.

Muslims (people who practice Islam) serve a god who loves humankind **conditionally**.

The god of Islam loves only those who follow him and contribute to his cause:

> ***Say, If ye love Allah, follow me; Allah will love you and forgive you your sins. (Surah 3:31, Qur'an)***
>
> ***Spend your wealth for the cause of Allah, and be not cast by your own hands to ruin; and do good. Lo! Allah loveth the beneficent. (Surah 2:135, Qur'an)***

Christians believe there is only one God who created the universe and is actively involved in the lives of its inhabitants. The Bible, God's Word, tells us that God is a God of love and grace: He saves us because of His *merciful love* for us. We are God's sons and daughters because in His love He has brought us into His family through the life, death, and resurrection of His Son, Jesus, rather than through our own work or sacrifice, which is what the other monotheistic religions teach.

Why would Jesus want to die for us?

Throughout the Qur'an (the Islamic "bible"), we read that Allah (the Islamic god) loves those who do good and does not love those who do evil. Allah is not at all like the Christian God who ...

Demonstrates His own love for us in this: While we were still sinners, Christ died for us. (Romans 5:8)

This is how God showed His love among us: He sent His one and only Son into the world that we might live through Him. This is love: not that we loved God, but that He loved us and sent His Son as an atoning sacrifice for our sins. (1 John 4:9-10)

John Gilchrist's online article, "The Love of God in the Qur'an and the Bible," states:

The Qur'an does not give the believer any total assurance of the forgiveness of all his sins this side of the grave. Accordingly it is hardly surprising that it sets the prospect of forgiveness at the end of life as the reward of service to God. Even then there is no complete assurance that the believer will be forgiven and the believer can only die in the hope of God's mercy. (Surah 17:57)

To put it in a nutshell, there is no definite expression of love in the heart of God towards men in the Qur'an. No proof of deep affection towards mankind is given at all.[25]

In contrast, Jesus tells Nicodemus:

"For God so loved the world that He gave His one and only Son, that whoever believes in Him shall not perish but have eternal life. For God did not send His Son into the world to condemn the world, but to save the world through Him." (John 3:16-17)

St. Paul writes of the Christian faith, “For it is by grace you have been saved, through faith—and this not from yourselves, it is the gift of God—not by works, so that no one can boast” (Ephesians 2:8–9).

We’ll talk more about the characteristics of the Christian God—our **one true God**—in chapters 10–13. We’ll also look at how our God is eager for a relationship with His creations in chapter 14.

After Walda Wood's husband, Tom, died at age 45, the businesswoman reported receiving messages from her late spouse. Tom's description of God and heaven appears on Walda's website.

> **He is made up of brilliant love, light, and energy. His wisdom is incomprehensible even to us who have been here awhile. We just know that to be in His presence is to become Him, blending with His greatness and feeling His love through an elation that has no human words to describe it. God blew the breath of life into Adam and created us all in His image. This is what connects us all as one. We all have that God part in our souls as many may know as the Grace of God. Mankind needs to stop viewing God as an entity outside of himself and start seeing Him as a loving force residing inside of himself.**

CHAPTER 8

Isn't God in Everything and in Everybody?

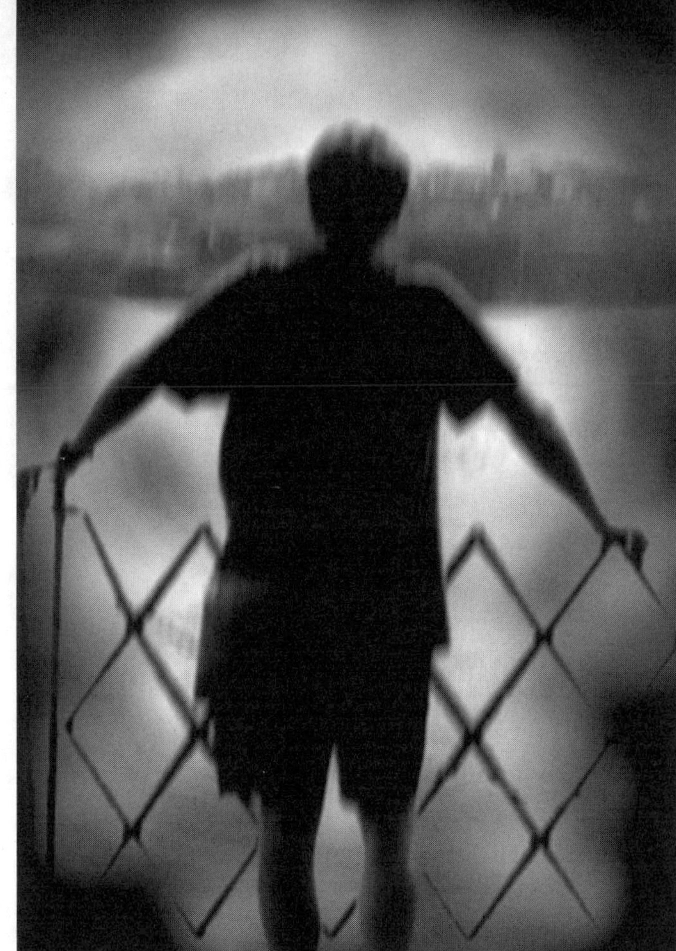

Heaven

is a state of consciousness—interwoven levels of energy and consciousness. It intermingles with your dimension but vibrates at a much higher frequency. As Jesus told His disciples, "The kingdom of Heaven is within you." When the physical body can no longer exist, it dies and the energy which makes up the soul and spirit continues on, in a state of consciousness that is eternal. Remember, "the soul has a body," not "the body has a soul." God gave man physical form to learn the concept of separateness. To die is only a matter of changing consciousness! To have an out-of-body experience while still living in the earth is very similar, only the "silver cord" which many speak of is not severed, allowing the astral consciousness to return to the body.[26]

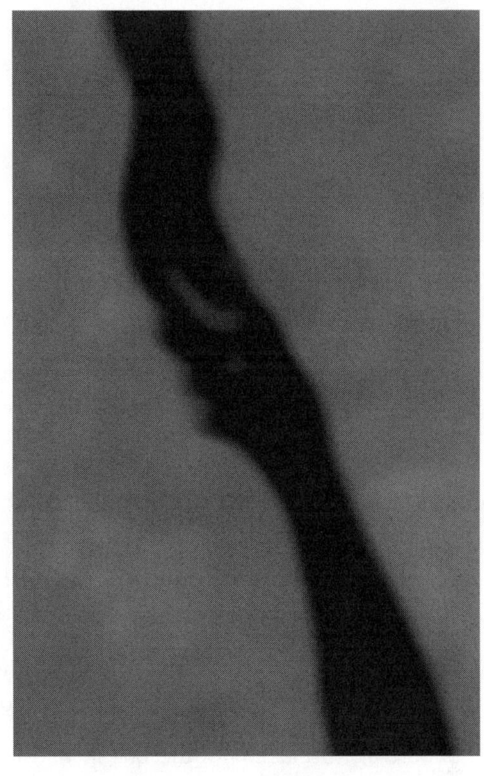

This idea that we are God and that God is us has been promoted by Shirley MacLaine and, more recently, by New Age physician and philosopher Deepak Chopra. His latest book, *How to Know God: The Soul's Journey into the Mystery of Mysteries,* "continues [Chopra's] pioneering outreach, showing that God consciousness ... and your own deepest Self ... are one and the same. Above all, it is about waking up to who we really are: infinite, immortal, eternal. God is the mirror in which we reveal ourselves to ourselves. We have made God in our own hearts."[27]

Chopra is also collecting material for a new book called *Messages from God.* According to his website, these messages, or "anomalous experiences," take the form of "sudden flashes of profound inspiration, insight, former lifetimes, telepathy, ESP, alter-ego, synchronicity, clairvoyance, prophecy, spontaneous healing, or miracles."

New Age concepts of God, however, are nothing new. If you've grown up in the church, you probably learned about them in Sunday school! It's all there in the story of Adam and Eve. The Bible records:

Now the serpent was more crafty than any of the wild animals the LORD God had made. He said to the woman, "Did God *really* say, 'You must not eat from any tree in the garden'?" (Genesis 3:1, italics mine)

New Age followers believe they can discover their own truth.

Modern reincarnationists try to avoid any judgment or analysis of their claims because as actress Shirley MacLaine writes, "Reality [is] only what one person perceive[s] it to be. Everyone's perception of reality [is] valid."[28]

In other words, because my friend Rob Holt believes Kosgro McOrlo Excelsior exists, it therefore exists. And he, she, or it is just as **real** as this computer I'm typing on—at least according to MacLaine. Then again, MacLaine wouldn't admit that this PC is real because she believes "reality [is] only what one believe[s] it to be anyway. That would make all perceived realities real."[29] Everything is "basically part of what we called 'God.'"[30]

So according to MacLaine, the questions of "proof" and "reliability" are irrelevant because there is no such thing as truth and falsehood, good or evil. People have their own truth, so it's not possible to judge another's truth.

That means there's no systematic New Age theology because its followers accept all philosophies as equally valid. In our schools, government, media, and many churches, we hear the echo from Eden, "There is no absolute **truth**. We can determine what's right and wrong for us. We have no right to judge one another." (Isn't it a bit illogical to be so absolute about there being no absolute truth?!) Since Eve first bit into the lie that God doesn't *really* expect us to follow His command, our world has reaped the bitter fruit of moral neutrality.

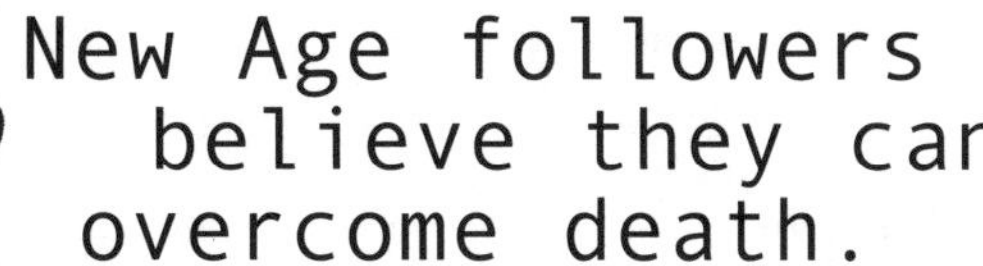
New Age followers
believe they can
overcome death.

Genesis 3 continues:

> The woman said to the serpent, "We may eat fruit from the trees in the garden, but God did say, 'You must not eat fruit from the tree that is in the middle of the garden, and you must not touch it, or you will die.'"
>
> "You will not surely die," the serpent said to the woman. (Genesis 3:2-4)

Rather than **hissed** by slippery serpents, today's false hopes are voiced by well-educated and best-selling authors. L. Ron Hubbard is the author of the best-selling book *Dianetics: The Modern Science of Mental Health* (16,000,000 copies sold) and the founder of Scientology. He believes a person is neither a body nor a mind, but a spiritual being, independent of both. This spiritual being uses the mind and body to interact with the physical universe.

James Redfield's best-selling *Celestine Prophecy* teaches "Nine Insights" for connecting to "God's energy in such a way that we will eventually become beings of light, and walk straight into heaven."[31]

Betty Eadie's best-selling book *Embraced by the Light* uses her "out-of-body experience" to serve up a casserole of Christianity, Eastern religion, and reincarnation. Briefly, reincarnation is the ultimate recycling project. Souls return to earth in various forms until they reach the highest level of consciousness. "Karma" controls this cosmic Chutes and Ladders game. (You can read more about reincarnation in *Is There Really Life after Death?*, the second book in this series.)

Reincarnationists believe humans begin on the low end of the food chain, but if they live a good life, they return as higher life-forms. The whole idea of karma, however, contradicts the first doctrine of New Age philosophy. With no rights or wrongs, how can one be judged? Perhaps some added illumination is needed, which brings us to New Age promise three:

New Age followers believe they can "expand" their consciousness.

The serpent continues,

> "For God knows that when you eat of it your eyes will be opened, ... knowing good and evil." (Genesis 3:5)

Because we are created in the image of God, there is something within us that senses there is **knowledge** beyond what we can see, hear, touch, taste, and smell. The New Age movement capitalizes on that God-given instinct for supernatural knowledge with books, tapes, and lectures promising "enlightenment."

Because all have "their own versions of enlightenment," the new spiritualists consult a variety of sources of "higher knowledge": astrology; out-of-body experiences; tarot cards; "I Ching," Chinese fortune-telling coins; prehistoric Native Americans who allegedly "channel" this age-old wisdom to receptive people of today; "angels"; Mother Nature; goddesses such as Sophia; and even visitors from other planets.

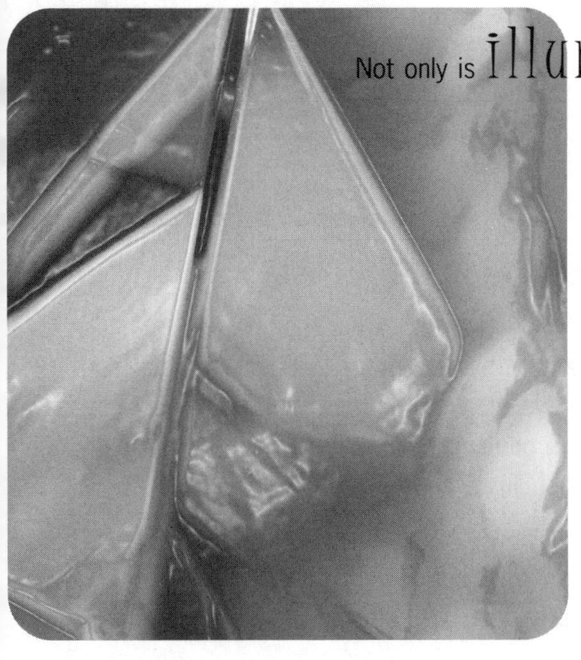

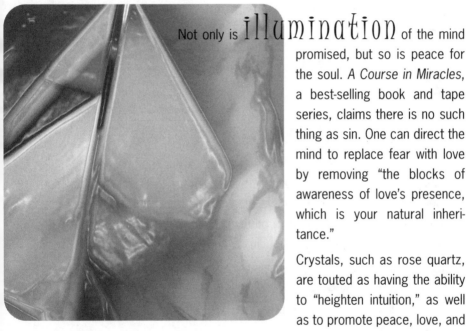

Not only is illumination of the mind promised, but so is peace for the soul. *A Course in Miracles*, a best-selling book and tape series, claims there is no such thing as sin. One can direct the mind to replace fear with love by removing "the blocks of awareness of love's presence, which is your natural inheritance."

Crystals, such as rose quartz, are touted as having the ability to "heighten intuition," as well as to promote peace, love, and self-acceptance. Topaz is marketed as providing "mental stimulation and creativity." (According to the New Age catalogs, there's a crystal for every emotional and spiritual need!)

For those in the New Age, whatever furthers one's enlightenment is enthusiastically accepted and embraced—no questions asked.

Is God simply in the lives of all believers, or all people, or all nature?

New Age followers believe they can become God.

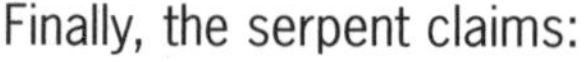

Finally, the serpent claims:

> "... and you will be like God ..." (Genesis 3:5)

The Mormons (Latter Day Saints) always have promised that the faithful can one day become gods. MacLaine's televised version of her book *Out on a Limb*, however, mainstreamed the idea. In one scene, the actress stands alone on a beach, arms lifted heavenward, shouting, "I am God! I am God! I am God!"

But the Mormons and MacLaine are not alone out there on the limb. Best-selling books and tapes by sought-after speakers promise to "Release the Divinity Within" and "discover the healing properties of the Higher Self."

Tragically,

> When the woman saw that the fruit of the tree was good for food and pleasing to the eye, and also desirable for gaining wisdom, she took some and ate it. She also gave some to her husband, who was with her, and he ate it. (Genesis 3:6)

That tragedy is multiplied by the millions who have bitten into the poisonous promises of spiritual insight and power apart from God.

Is there anything wrong with the New Age?

The serpent's offer was attractive because it seemed to promise the fulfillment of a legitimate desire—to know good and evil. But God had created Adam and Eve in His image—righteous, holy, and doing His will. They truly knew God and were happy with Him—even walking and talking with Him in the garden.

But Adam and Eve weren't satisfied. They wanted to be more than the crown of God's creation—they wanted to "be like God." In one bite, Adam and Eve (and all their human descendants) were separated from God and lost His image. Humans have tried many ways since that time to recapture God's image—and New Age philosophies offer delicious-looking solutions. But New Age teachings are satanic shortcuts to the goal of knowing good and evil. Only in God's Word do we learn about God's expectations, our inability to meet His expectations, and His gift of Jesus, who earned the forgiveness that brings us into the family of God.

Jesus proclaims, "I am the way and the truth and the life. No one comes to the Father except through Me" (John 14:6). Notice that Jesus doesn't offer us *a* way, *a* truth, and *a* life. He offers us Himself. No shortcuts, no easy answers! A cross rather than crystals. Servanthood in place of a "higher self." The life (eternal life) instead of a "light."

Slippery, slick serpents may have been replaced with smooth, sophisticated spokespersons, but the venom is just as deadly. That's why Jesus warns, "The thief comes only to steal and kill and destroy; I have come that they may have life, and have it to the full" (John 10:10).

My lockermate in junior high was always asking God to destroy the temperamental combination lock that made us late for class. Wouldn't it have been great fun if God had taken Keith's request seriously? Suddenly thunder, lightning—then only a *wisp* of smoke where the lock had been. That would have gotten people's attention. That would have convinced students that God existed, right? Somehow, I don't think that it would convince them of His existence if God took people's swearing seriously.

CHAPTER 9 How Do You Know There Is a God?

The Egyptians didn't seem too impressed when God turned all their water to blood; sent in an army of frogs, gnats, flies, and locusts; killed off all their livestock; gave them all boils; pounded them with hailstones; and turned out the lights. And that was just the first nine plagues. Even the Israelites forgot about God parting the Red Sea and setting off a fireworks display at Mount Sinai. Maybe that's why God's **miracles** have occurred only in three or four periods of history. (We'll talk about miracles in chapter 17.)

Can we see God?

If God isn't sending fire and brimstone on unsuspecting combination locks or sinful cities, how does He reveal Himself to us today?

Through Nature

Every culture has been aware of some supreme being as revealed in *nature.* Psalm 19 states, "The heavens declare the glory of God; the skies proclaim the work of His hands" (19:1). The apostle Paul writes:

> The wrath of God is being revealed from heaven against all the godlessness and wickedness of men who suppress the truth by their wickedness, since what may be known about God is plain to them, because God has made it plain to them. For since the creation of the world God's invisible qualities—His eternal power and divine nature—have been clearly seen, being understood from what has been made, so that men are without excuse. (Romans 1:18-20)

I remember thinking, *Wow! What a cool God we have!* while in biology class in a secular high school. Mr. Ruble had spent the first part of the semester talking about how we had evolved from **amino acid chains**, which turned into proteins, and then one-celled organisms, and—give or take three or four billion years—human beings.

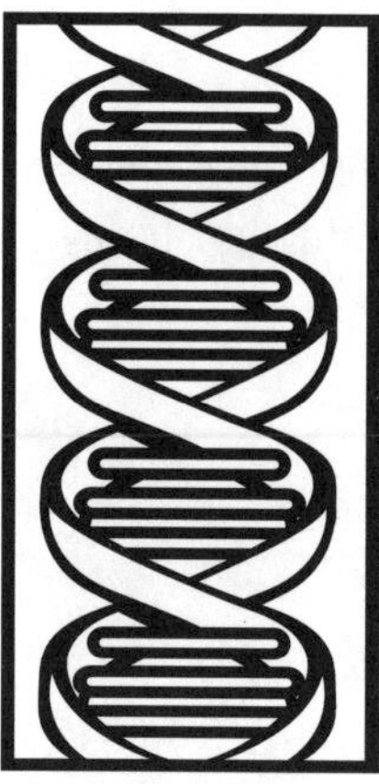

Okay, I could buy the argument that "every event or change must have a sufficient and pre-existing cause" and that "the universe consists of a system of changes." But as Mr. Ruble began to teach about the human body, I simply didn't have enough faith to believe that we were all some kind of cosmic **accident**. Our biology book didn't have an answer for the "pre-existing cause." Besides, the second law of thermodynamics states that things tend to go from complex to simple, not from simple to complex. (Leave a banana in your locker over Christmas break and you'll discover that physics principle firsthand!)

So I began to consider the human eye. If the theory of evolution were true, the retina would have appeared as a genetic mutation. Then, because the mutants could survive better with a retina, they would multiply more than non-retina creatures. Then more **mutations** would create a lens; then after another billion years, a pupil with an adjustable iris would develop, then a cornea; and eventually, organisms with eyes would overtake all the other organisms bumping into predators in the dark.

But for an eye to work—and thus provide survival advantage—wouldn't you need a complete eye?! Bits and pieces of an eye won't be more advantageous than no eye at all. We need a clever designer to create in an instant fully functioning eyes with binocular vision, muscles to move them, tear ducts to lubricate the corneas, not to mention a **complex** brain to interpret the optical signals.

And that's just an eye! Such a marvelous design certainly seems to need an intelligent designer. For me, it takes less faith to believe in a Creator than to believe evolution, chance, and natural selection created our incredibly complex bodies, not to mention our brains!

Unfortunately, many choose to ignore the evidence from nature for an intelligent Creator. Paul continues:

> For although they knew God, they neither glorified Him as God nor gave thanks to Him, but their thinking became futile and their foolish hearts were darkened. Although they claimed to be wise, they became fools. (Romans 1:21-22)

Through the Prophets

So God sent *prophets* to explain who He was. But despite Elijah calling down fire from heaven and performing other really cool miracles, people just didn't get it. Even when God gave His messengers prophetic messages that—contrary to those of *The National Enquirer*—actually came to fulfillment precisely as predicted, humans were still unimpressed.

In fact, the prophets "... faced jeers and flogging, while still others were chained and put in prison. They were stoned; they were sawed in two; they were put to death by the sword. They went about in sheepskins and goatskins, destitute, persecuted and mistreated ..." (Hebrews 11:36–37). Not exactly a successful speaking tour!

So how do you—if you're God—communicate to your human creations?

Will we ever be able to comprehend everything about God?

To answer that, let's pretend your dog is watching you read the newspaper. This totally confuses Rover because all he understands about *newspaper* is "house-breaking." *Duh, why are you sitting there staring at* toilet paper *when you could be outside chasing cars or rolling in something really smelly?!*

Humans just don't make sense!

Of course, it doesn't make sense to a creature with a brain the size of a tennis ball! We humans, however, can take little black ink spots on white paper and communicate thoughts to one another—just like we're doing right now. I'm converting my thoughts into keystrokes on my computer, which will be saved as "on" and "off" signals on a floppy disk. Those will be downloaded onto a printing plate, which will produce the very book you're reading. Amazing! And totally unbelievable and inconceivable to your dog. Just try to explain it to Rover.

That's why the apostle Paul calls God and His love for us a "mystery" 50 times in his letters. Nature was inadequate to express God's character fully.

Through Jesus, His Son

God's solution to communicating with His human creations might appear absolutely outrageous: He became a human to communicate with humans. (That would be like you becoming a dog to explain newspapers to Rover!)

> He is the image of the invisible God, the first-born over all creation. For by Him all things were created: things in heaven and on earth, visible and invisible, whether thrones or powers or rulers or authorities; all things were created by Him and for Him. He is before all things, and in Him all things hold together. And He is the head of the body, the church; He is the

beginning and the firstborn from among the dead, so that in everything He might have the supremacy. For God was pleased to have all His fullness dwell in Him. (Colossians 1:15-19)

How can God be Jesus' "Father" if Jesus is God in human form?

The amazing thing is that Jesus is both **true God and true man**—in one person (Colossians 2:9). But there are three persons in God—which is why we call God "the Trinity." So Jesus is the Son of God the Father.

We'll talk more about the three persons of God—the Father, the Son, and the Holy Spirit—in separate chapters later.

Can you really encounter something supernatural?

If you're taking notes, here's the main point: Nature gives us a glimpse of God's power and creativity. The prophets point us to God and reveal His divine attributes—all-knowing (who else can accurately predict the future?), all-powerful (who else can rouse the dead?), loving, and so much more. And in Jesus we see God in human form, revealing His gracious love for us. Because of Jesus' life, death, and resurrection, we are able to know God as our loving Father, our Brother, and the one who works faith in our hearts. The one, true, living God reveals Himself as

Creator,

Savior,

and **Comforter.**

Who created God?

CHAPTER

10 What Is God Like?

We talked in the previous chapter about how God's mental powers are infinitely greater than ours as our minds are greater than those of our pets. The mere concept of God seems totally unbelievable and inconceivable to us. So how do you answer: Where did God come from? How old is God? How could He always have been? How does God count time?

I have no clue how God always could have been with no beginning and no end. (I'm getting a headache just thinking about it!) I might as well try to explain reading to Rover than try to **comprehend** an eternal being!

The prophet Isaiah writes:

> "For My thoughts are not your thoughts, neither are your ways My ways," declares the LORD. "As the heavens are higher than the earth, so are My ways higher than your ways and My thoughts than your thoughts." (Isaiah 55:8-9)

And Paul writes:

> Oh, the depth of the riches of the wisdom and knowledge of God! How unsearchable His judgments, and His paths beyond tracing out! "Who has known the mind of the Lord? Or who has been His counselor?" "Who has ever given to God, that God should repay him?" For from Him and through Him and to Him are all things. To Him be the glory forever! Amen. (Romans 11:33-36)
>
> For the foolishness of God is wiser than man's wisdom, and the weakness of God is stronger than man's strength. (1 Corinthians 1:25)

Because the concept of God is way beyond me, I'll let Him talk for Himself in this chapter. I've simply arranged what He has to say for Himself through

His Word.

God's Attributes (Characteristics)

Does God have a body

or

is He like a big humongous spirit?

God is an eternal spirit

God is spirit. (John 4:24)

For this is what the high and lofty One says—He who lives forever, whose name is holy. (Isaiah 57:15a)

Now to the King eternal, immortal, invisible, the only God, be honor and glory for ever and ever. Amen. (1 Timothy 1:17)

How old is God?

Before the mountains were born or You brought forth the earth and the world, from everlasting to everlasting You are God. (Psalm 90:2)

"I am the Alpha and the Omega," says the Lord God, "who is, and who was, and who is to come, the Almighty." (Revelation 1:8)

God is present everywhere
(omnipresent)

"The heavens, even the highest heavens, cannot contain You." (2 Chronicles 6:18b)

"Can anyone hide in secret places so that I cannot see him?" declares the LORD. "Do not I fill heaven and earth?" declares the LORD. (Jeremiah 23:24)

How can the Holy Spirit be with everybody at one time?

He is not far from each one of us. (Acts 17:27)

Where can I go from Your Spirit? Where can I flee from Your presence? If I go up to the heavens, You are there; if I make my bed in the depths, You are there. If I rise on the wings of the dawn, if I settle on the far side of the sea, even there Your hand will guide me, Your right hand will hold me fast. (King David in Psalm 139:7-9)

God is all-knowing
(omniscient)

Lord, You know all things. (John 21:17)

Nothing in all creation is hidden from God's sight. Everything is uncovered and laid bare before the eyes of Him to whom we must give account. (Hebrews 4:13)

"To God belong wisdom and power; counsel and understanding are His." (Job 12:13)

God ... knows everything. (1 John 3:20)

God is all-powerful
(omnipotent)

"O Sovereign LORD, You have begun to show to Your servant Your greatness and Your strong hand. For what god is there in heaven or on earth who can do the deeds and mighty works You do?" (Deuteronomy 3:24)

"Ah, Sovereign LORD, You have made the heavens and the earth by Your great power and outstretched arm. Nothing is too hard for You." (Jeremiah 32:17)

Our God is in heaven; He does whatever pleases Him. (Psalm 115:3)

With God all things are possible. (Matthew 19:26)

Then Jesus came to them and said, "All authority in heaven and on earth has been given to Me." (Matthew 28:18)

God is changeless

"I the LORD do not change." (Malachi 3:6)

Every good and perfect gift is from above, coming down from the Father of the heavenly lights, who does not change like shifting shadows. (James 1:17)

God is holy

There is no one holy like the LORD. (1 Samuel 2:2)

I, the LORD your God, am holy. (Leviticus 19:2)

Holy, holy, holy is the LORD Almighty. (Isaiah 6:3)

God is just
(fair, impartial)

You are not a God who takes pleasure in evil; with You the wicked cannot dwell.... You hate all who do wrong. (Psalm 5:4-5)

The LORD is slow to anger and great in power; the LORD will not leave the guilty unpunished. (Nahum 1:3)

He is the Rock, His works are perfect, and all His ways are just. A faithful God who does no wrong, upright and just is He. (Deuteronomy 32:4)

God is love

Dear friends, let us love one another, for love comes from God. Everyone who loves has been born of God and knows God. Whoever does not love does not know God, because God is love. This is how God showed His love among us: He sent His one and only Son into the world that we might live through Him. This is love: not that we loved God, but that He loved us and sent His Son as an atoning sacrifice for our sins. (1 John 4:7–10)

God is gracious
(showing undeserved kindness, forgiving)

The LORD, the LORD, the compassionate and gracious God, slow to anger, abounding in love and faithfulness, maintaining love to thousands, and forgiving wickedness, rebellion and sin. (Exodus 34:6–7)

The LORD is gracious and righteous; our God is full of compassion. (Psalm 116:5)

For God so loved the world that He gave His one and only Son, that whoever believes in Him shall not perish but have eternal life. (John 3:16)

The LORD is not slow in keeping His promise, as some understand slowness. He is patient with you, not wanting anyone to perish, but everyone to come to repentance. (2 Peter 3:9)

God is faithful

If we are faithless, He will remain faithful, for He cannot disown Himself. (2 Timothy 2:13)

Know therefore that the LORD your God is God; He is the faithful God, keeping His covenant of love to a thousand generations of those who love Him and keep His commands. (Deuteronomy 7:9)

God is not a man, that He should lie, nor a son of man, that He should change His mind. Does He speak and then not act? Does He promise and not fulfill? (Numbers 23:19)

God is our refuge and strength, an ever-present help in trouble. (Psalm 46:1)

Surely God is my help; the LORD is the one who sustains me. (Psalm 54:4)

"The LORD your God is with you, He is mighty to save. He will take great delight in you, He will quiet you with His love, He will rejoice over you with singing." (Zephaniah 3:17)

God is merciful
(full of pity)

The LORD our God is merciful and forgiving, even though we have rebelled against Him. (Daniel 9:9)

"I am merciful," declares the LORD. (Jeremiah 3:12)

He saved us, not because of righteous things we had done, but because of His mercy. (Titus 3:5)

God is good

Your righteousness reaches to the skies, O God, You who have done great things. Who, O God, is like You? (Psalm 71:19)

How great is Your goodness. (Psalm 31:19)

Give thanks to the LORD, for He is good; His love endures forever. (Psalm 118:1)

The LORD is righteous in all His ways and loving toward all He has made. (Psalm 145:17)

All of these **attributes** (and many more) describe God perfectly. And God uses them perfectly in His interaction with His human creations. Which is a good thing. Here's a story to help you understand.

Mike Morris was quick to anger and great in power. He ruled the first-grade playground with his wannabe gang members. Since he had been held back in kindergarten, Mike had a physical advantage that allowed him to bully his way to the front of any line, eat the chocolate chip cookies right out of your lunchbox, and do whatever he decided he wanted to do.

Eugene Scott also was quick to anger. But he was shorter and 10 pounds lighter than any of the Morris mob, so he spent a lot of time in the nurse's office with an icepack over his mouth and/or eye.

Then there was me. I had a longer fuse than Eugene, but I was also skinnier than any of the recess rebels. I spent most of my time trying to be where Mike and his posse weren't.

Our only salvation was Mr. Grimes, the principal. He never raised his voice. He rarely smiled, but he rarely frowned either—he just had sort of an I'm-in-charge-here stare. And when Mr. Grimes silently

patrolled the playground, Mike and his mob quickly moved to the back of the line, returned stolen cookies, and appeared to be model first-graders.

I'm glad Mr. Grimes had not only power, but patience as well. More important, I'm glad that God *is not like* a Mike Morris, a Eugene Scott, or a Jim Watkins. God has absolute power and shows unconditional love in Jesus, our Lord. If He were all power and not love, we'd all be dead! If He were all love and no power, we'd be living with a "Barney the Dinosaur" God. And His love and power are exercised with unlimited wisdom. "Great is our Lord and mighty in power; His understanding has no limit" (Psalm 147:5).

Most evangelical Christian churches teach "that the one true God is the Father and the Son and the Holy [Spirit], three distinct persons, but of one and the same divine essence, equal in power, equal in eternity, equal in majesty, because each person possesses the [entire] one divine essence ..."[32]

What's the Trinity all about?

CHAPTER 11

Aren't the Father, Son, and Holy Spirit All the Same?

The Bible states there is one—and **only one**—God. In fact, the ancient Hebrew nation held as the highest commandment belief in this one God: "Hear, O Israel: The LORD our God, the LORD is one. Love the LORD your God with all your heart and with all your soul and with all your strength" (Deuteronomy 6:4–5). And Jesus Himself reiterates this commandment in one of His discussions with a teacher of the law (Mark 12:29–32).

So are there three different Gods?

However, God refers to Himself in the plural in the first chapter of the Bible: "Let *Us* make man in *Our* image, in *Our* likeness" (Genesis 1:26). From the beginning, we understand that God is somehow one God in three distinct persons. Some theologians have mistakenly tried to explain the Trinity by saying that God revealed Himself in three separate forms: God the Father, God the Son (Jesus Christ), and God the Holy Spirit. Yet at Jesus' baptism, all three persons are present:

> When all the people were being baptized, Jesus was baptized too. And as He was praying, heaven was opened and the Holy Spirit descended on Him in bodily form like a dove. And a voice came from heaven: "You are My Son, whom I love; with You I am well pleased." (Luke 3:21-22)

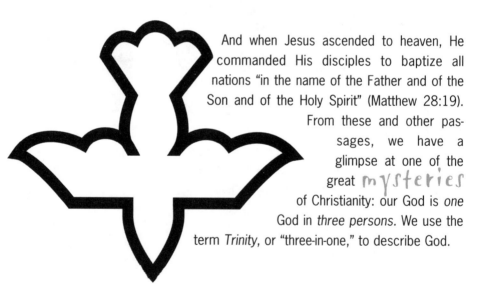

And when Jesus ascended to heaven, He commanded His disciples to baptize all nations "in the name of the Father and of the Son and of the Holy Spirit" (Matthew 28:19). From these and other passages, we have a glimpse at one of the great mysteries of Christianity: our God is *one* God in *three persons*. We use the term *Trinity*, or "three-in-one," to describe God.

Is God the Son the same as God the Father?

Some religious thinkers have attempted to explain the Three-in-One as being *like* electricity, which is one force that can be expressed as heat (an electric heater), light (a light bulb), and motion (an electric motor). As an electric heater, a light bulb, and an electric motor are distinctly separate "things," so God the Son, God the Father, and God the Holy Spirit are distinct persons within the Godhead—the one God. The analogy breaks down, however, because the light bulb does create motion in the sense of light waves, the heater may produce some light, the motor probably produces some heat. The three persons of the Trinity all possess the same attributes or qualities (see chapter 10) but have **unique** identities as God.

For millennia, the brightest religious thinkers have attempted to explain the Trinity. But just as we said it would appear impossible to explain a newspaper to your dog, we run into problems again and again as we try to grasp completely our Triune God.

Would the Father be considered the "leader" of the Trinity?

Jesus makes reference many times to being obedient to the Father's plan, but these references are always made when He is speaking of His distinct role as Savior of sinful human beings. God the Father sent His only Son to this earth to accomplish our salvation. This required that Jesus lay aside His full power and glory, taking on human form (Philippians 2:6–8; Hebrews 2:14). In this sense, He subjected or made Himself obedient to God the Father.

"The world must learn that I love the Father and that I do exactly what My Father has commanded Me." (John 14:31)

"Father, if You are willing, take this cup from Me; yet not My will, but Yours be done." (Luke 22:42)

Is the Holy Spirit as important as Jesus or God the Father?

Before Jesus died, He told His disciples that He was returning to "Him who sent Me" and that He would send the Counselor (Holy Spirit) to them (John 16:5–16). From this passage, we know that the **Holy Spirit** is sent by God the Father and God the Son to work in the lives of humans. We know from other passages that the special work of the Holy Spirit is to sanctify or make holy (1 Corinthians 6:11). He works faith in our hearts as we listen to the Gospel (1 Corinthians 12:3).

As you can see, it's pretty difficult to wrap our human minds around the concept of the **Triune God**. As one writer said, "There is no analogy, no simile, no illustration in the wide realm of human thought which could clarify for us this profound mystery. ... The finite mind of man simply cannot comprehend the infinite God."[33] But even this small understanding of our wondrous God reveals the immensity of His power, love, and grace in our lives.

This is sacrilegious, I thought. My 4-year-old son had taken his World Wrestling Federation action figure and had fastened him to a wooden cross with rubber bands creating a National Endowment for the Arts version of the crucifix.

CHAPTER

12 Did Jesus Have a Girlfriend?

This "Jesus" had muscles on top of muscles—pecs the size of couch cushions; black, curly hair; and a Coppertone tan. This was not the **cardboard cutout** Jesus from Sunday school class or the stereotype from the movies. The Hollywood "Jesus" looks like he stepped off the cover of a romance best-seller: blow-dried auburn hair with blonde highlights, immaculately manicured nails, a pure white robe, and, of course, heavenly good looks.

But wait. Maybe my son's "action figure" Jesus is closer to the original.

What did Jesus look like?

First, Jesus was Jewish—not white Anglo-Saxon. Because this was before the days of extra-strength antiperspirant and stain-removing detergent, His robe probably had sweat rings, and His curly black hair didn't **glisten** from a recent hot oil treatment. And He may have had muscles—at least enough brawn to bounce the money changers out of the temple.

But worse than what artists and movie producers have done with the physical characteristics of Jesus is what some theologians, church leaders, and revisionist historians have done to who the Bible reveals Jesus to be! Let's take a look at the differences between the **genuine Christ** and the counterfeit articles.

Counterfeit Christs Are Either All Man or All God; the **Genuine Christ** Is **True Man** and **True God**

Most cults can be identified by how they view Christ. For example,

- "Christian" Science believes Jesus is merely a grand "spiritual idea."
- Jehovah's Witnesses teach that Jesus is not God incarnate but "no more than a perfect man." His resurrection was spiritual, so "the man Jesus is dead, dead forever."

☆ Mormon leader Brigham Young declared that God "was once a man in mortal flesh as we are, and is now an exalted being." Thus Christ was simply a human on His way to godhood.

☆ Sun Myung Moon, the founder of the Unification Church, believes that the priest Zacharias was the father of Jesus, thus Christ was "a human being and not a supernatural person." Moon believes *he* is the messiah!

☆ Other groups believe Jesus was only 100 percent God because God—and God alone—can forgive our sins and remain sinless Himself.

Was Jesus a part of God?

Jesus is the world's only 100 percent being who is 100 percent God ***and*** 100 percent human. It's another one of those "God things" that doesn't make any sense to our earthly brains.

The Bible says Jesus is truly, completely God. The apostle John begins his gospel by referring to Jesus as *the Word*. "In the beginning was the Word, and the Word was with God, and the Word was God" (John 1:1). Jesus is called "our great God and Savior" by the apostle Paul (Titus 2:13).

Paul also writes, "He is the image of the invisible God ... . For God was pleased to have all His fullness dwell in Him" (Colossians 1:15, 19). The word *image* in Greek is *eikon*. (You really don't have to remember that, unless you're a contestant on *Jeopardy*.) The word means more than just a representation; it means a *manifestation*. J.B. Phillips translates this phrase as "the visible expression of the invisible God." Jesus **is** God made visible.

Jesus Himself declares, "I and the Father are one" (John 10:30). Plus, He accepts (and even demands) worship as God when He says, "... honor the Son just as they honor the Father. He who does not honor the Son does not honor the Father, who sent Him" (John 5:23). And Jesus has "authority on earth to forgive sins" (Luke 5:24).

Jesus' actions back up His words: He *heals* the sick, **multiplies** loaves and fishes, controls weather, **tells** stormy seas to be still, and *raises* the dead—repeatedly! Obviously, no human can do those things!

But the Bible also says Jesus is completely human. "There is one God and one mediator between God and men, the *man* Christ Jesus" (1 Timothy 2:5, italics mine).

Was Jesus really a man? Was Jesus an angel?

Jesus was born to a human mother, Mary—though it's pretty amazing to have a mother who is a virgin (Luke 1:26–38)! Jesus developed physically as well as socially and mentally: "And Jesus grew in wisdom and stature, and in favor with God and men" (Luke 2:52).

Unfortunately, we have no biblical record of what Jesus did from age 12 to approximately age 30. And when He did do something miraculous as an adult, His family "went to take charge of Him, for they said, 'He is out of His mind'" (Mark 3:21).

How did Jesus know He was God's Son?

At 12, Jesus amazed the top theologians of the time at the temple. And when asked by His earthly parents why He had not accompanied them back to Nazareth, Jesus told them, "Didn't you know I had to be in *My Father's* house?" (Luke 2:49b). From this passage, we know Jesus always knew He was **God's Son.**

Did Jesus eat and drink like a regular person?

When Jesus was on earth, was He ever tempted to sin?

Jesus, the man, became thirsty, hungry, tired, frustrated, and sorrowful. And Scripture reveals that Jesus wasn't tempted only in the wilderness for 40 days (Matthew 4:1–11), but at other "opportune" times as well (Luke 4:13), especially during His walk to the cross.

So we can see from these and many more references that Jesus was both God and man. According to Hebrews 4:15, we have a Savior who can "sympathize with our weaknesses [for He] has been tempted in every way, just as we are—yet was without sin." (Remember C.S. Lewis's quote from chapter 6 that Jesus is either "Lord, liar, or lunatic"!)

Counterfeit Christs Emphasize Law; the **Genuine Christ** Emphasizes **Love**

The Pharisees—the religious leaders of Palestine—kept hundreds of human laws and regulations so they could be "righteous." The **genuine Christ**, however, summarized God's Law in two commandments:

> Jesus replied: "'Love the Lord your God with all your heart and with all your soul and with all your mind.' This is the first and greatest commandment. And the second is like it: 'Love your neighbor as yourself.' All the Law and the Prophets hang on these two commandments." (Matthew 22:37-40)

Jesus also gave His disciples a special command:

> "A new command I give you: Love one another. As I have loved you, so you must love one another. By this all men will know that you are My disciples, if you love one another." (John 13:34-35)

Although Jesus gave us these commands, He knew we wouldn't be able to obey them. Only He obeyed them perfectly. Then in His great love for us, He went to the **cross** to take our punishment for the times we break these laws. It is through His death that the greatest love of all—the love God has for sinners—is poured out. Jesus' death earned forgiveness for all our sins. His blood washes us and makes us clean. His sacrifice of love brings us into God's family. The Law no longer holds power over us (Romans 6:14).

Did Jesus have a girlfriend?

Although we have no biblical record of Jesus having a girlfriend, He did have female followers: Mary Magdalene, Joanna, Susanna, and "many

others" (Luke 8:3). We also know that Jesus interacted with women. He talked to the Samaritan woman He met at Jacob's well, which didn't go over well with some people. Because she was a *Samaritan,* "good" Jews avoided her. And to make matters worse, she had had a couple husbands and was currently living with a man who wasn't her husband. According to Jewish law, Jesus should have avoided her. But Jesus came to **save the lost**, including this woman, so He taught her about "springs of living water welling up to eternal life" (John 4:3–26).

During the time that Jesus lived, laws kept people from touching a leper or a dead body. Jesus routinely not only touched, but healed those with leprosy, and He raised the dead as well. Jesus also broke manmade laws about ceremonially washing before eating, doing anything other than breathing on the Sabbath, and worst of all, eating and drinking with tax collectors and "sinners."

The counterfeit Christs and their followers have long lists of "dos and don'ts" that are preached as "gospel." And everyone who didn't (or doesn't) subscribe to these legalistic lists is condemned.

Followers of the genuine Christ may not agree with the lifestyles and opinions of everyone (in fact, they shouldn't). But Christians will be the first to show *compassion* to those with whom they disagree. That's why Jesus hung out with drunks, prostitutes, tax collectors, and "sinners." He loved people. He didn't love their sinful actions—and didn't join them in those sinful behaviors—but He showed them that He loved them. He came to suffer and die for those sins and give to these sinners—and to us—forgiveness and new life. Followers of Jesus are not "preaching against" people with addictions; they are volunteering at rehabilitation programs at local shelters. They're not bombing abortion clinics; they're working in the pro-life Crisis Pregnancy Centers.

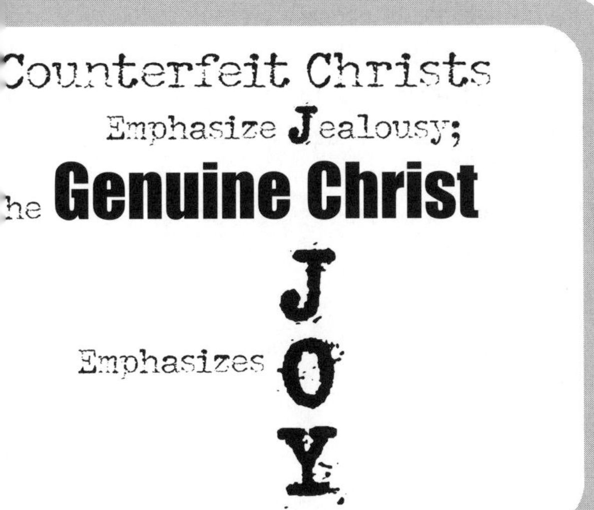
Counterfeit Christs
Emphasize Jealousy;
the Genuine Christ
Emphasizes
JOY

Have you noticed how some followers of Christ jealously guard their positions and perks, whether they are elders, pastors, or denominational executives? They insist on being referred to as "Elder Jones," "Reverend Smith," or "Doctor Brown." They enjoy the **reserved** parking spots, the large offices, and the sense of honor bestowed by those "below" them in the church.

Not the genuine Christ! He condemned the Pharisees' status seeking and egocentric attitudes. He told them that to become great, one should become a servant to all. Followers of the genuine Christ have a **Spirit-given** sense of joy and satisfaction in who they are—at whatever "level" on the social or ecclesiastical ladder they may find themselves. As Paul writes, we are freed to "serve one another in love" (Galatians 5:13).

Did Jesus have fun when He was on earth? Did Jesus like to tell jokes?

Jesus said, "I have told you this so that My joy may be in you and that your joy may be complete" (John 15:11). Jesus said these words as He was telling His disciples how much He loved them. What a great feeling—Jesus love us *and* He wants us to be joyful because He rejoices in us.

Jesus didn't just *talk* about joy, He brought joy to people's lives. He raised a widow's only son. He healed blind Bartimaeus. He fed the crowds. He saved His disciples on the stormy lake. He blessed the children. These are only a sampling of all Jesus did to **bring joy** to people through His earthly ministry. But think of the tremendous joy Mary felt on Easter morning to hear her risen Savior say her name. Or think of the joy the disciples felt as Jesus blessed them and commissioned them to spread the Gospel to all nations.

John Wesley claimed, "Sour religion is the devil's religion." Followers of Christ are filled with joy because they know they were created, loved, and forgiven of all sins by the God of the universe who sent His Son to die for them to create that relationship.

Counterfeit Christs Emphasize Politics; the **Genuine Christ** Emphasizes PEACE

Have you been turned off by a church group where crucifying politicians is more popular than proclaiming the crucified Christ? That group of believers may be following a counterfeit Christ. And if the TV preacher spends most of his time attacking those who don't follow his particular brand of theology, then he's probably not preaching the genuine Christ either.

Jesus spoke to a people dominated by the **political** corruption of false religious leaders and the Roman occupation. But He never once organized a **political action committee** or sent out one voting record score sheet of the Jewish High Council or Roman Imperial Senate. Instead, He spoke about peace.

> "Peace I leave with you; My peace I give you. I do not give to you as the world gives. Do not let your hearts be troubled and do not be afraid." (John 14:27)

> "I have told you these things, so that in Me you may have peace. In this world you will have trouble. But take heart! I have overcome the world." (John 16:33)

Jesus also spoke of **unity**—not pew politics or doctrinal debates.

> "My prayer is not for them alone. I pray also for those who will believe in Me through their message, that all of them may be one, Father, just as You are in Me and I am in You. May they also be in Us so that the world may believe that You have sent Me. I have given them the glory that You gave Me, that they may be one as We are one: I in them and You in Me. May they be brought

to complete unity to let the world know that You sent Me and have loved them even as You have loved Me." (John 17:20-23)

Because humans are involved in churches, there will always be doctrinal differences, but St. Paul urges Christians, "Make every effort to keep the unity of the Spirit through the bond of peace. There is one body [of Christ] and one Spirit—just as you were called to one hope when you were called—one Lord, one faith, one baptism; one God and Father of all, who is over all and through all and in all" (Ephesians 4:3–6).

If you want to learn more about the genuine Christ, explore for yourself the four books in the New Testament that record the life of Christ and His teachings—Matthew, Mark, Luke, and John. (Read from a modern translation such as *The New International Version, The New Revised Standard*, or *The New Living Translation*—they're easier to understand.) You'll discover that **your Savior** is real, honest, and authentic, and not at all like the caricatures of Him we often see in the theater, on television, and—unfortunately—in some of today's churches.

“Praise Father, Son, and Holy Ghost.”

Many churches sing “The Doxology” as a part of their service. As a child, I could understand the idea that God was like a father in His love and care for us all. And it made sense that if God was a father, He'd have to have at least one child. But the idea of a “Holy Ghost” gave me the creeps. After all, ghosts are intent on scaring the daylights out of people.

CHAPTER 13

Exactly Who Is the Holy Spirit?

How old is the Holy Spirit?

Is He a like a ghost?

What is He or She?

In the second verse of Genesis, we find “the Spirit of God” hovering over the yet-to-be-formed earth (Genesis 1:2). Throughout the Old Testament, we find references to God's prophets or messengers being inspired and empowered by His **Spirit**. In Isaiah and in many places in the New Testament, the Spirit of God is called by name: “the Holy Spirit” (Isaiah 63:10–11; Luke 1:35). (Remember from chapter 3, it's the Holy *Spirit*, not Holy Ghost!)

The Holy Spirit in the form of a dove descends on Jesus Christ at His baptism (Matthew 3:16). The Spirit empowers and emboldens the early disciples to preach the Good News (Acts 2:4)—the same disciples who had hidden behind locked doors after Jesus' crucifixion. And the Holy Spirit works and sustains faith in individuals (1 Corinthians 2:14; 2 Thessalonians 2:13–14).

What does the Holy Spirit do?

In Jesus Christ's farewell message to His disciples, He promised that He would send the Holy Spirit to His disciples.

> [Jesus told His disciples,] "I tell you the truth: It is for your good that I am going away. Unless I go away, the Counselor will not come to you; but if I go, I will send Him to you." (John 16:7)

The Holy Spirit convinces us of our need for a Savior

> "When He comes, He will convict the world of guilt in regard to sin and righteousness and judgment." (John 16:8)

The Holy Spirit works faith in believers

More than just convincing us of our need for the Savior, the Holy Spirit **opens** our hearts and minds to the truth that Jesus is our Savior and that, through faith in Him, we have forgiveness of sins and eternal life (1 Corinthians 2:14). The Holy Spirit works that faith in our hearts as we listen to God's Word, and He strengthens that faith as we take part in Baptism and the Lord's Supper.

Does He live inside of us?

The Holy Spirit lives within us

"And I will ask the Father, and He will give you another Counselor to be with you forever—the Spirit of truth. ... He lives with you and will be in you." (John 14:16-17)

The Holy Spirit teaches us God's truth

"But the Counselor, the Holy Spirit, whom the Father will send in My name, will teach you all things and will remind you of everything I have said to you." (John 14:26)

The Holy Spirit assures believers that they have been made children of God

The Spirit Himself testifies with our spirit that we are God's children. (Romans 8:16)

The Holy Spirit prays on behalf of believers

In the same way, the Spirit helps us in our weakness. We do not know what we ought to pray for, but the Spirit Himself intercedes for us with groans that words cannot express. And He who searches our hearts knows the mind of the Spirit, because the Spirit intercedes for the saints in accordance with God's will. (Romans 8:26-27)

The Holy Spirit transforms believers into Christlike people

The fruit of the Spirit is love, joy, peace, patience, kindness, goodness, faithfulness, gentleness and self-control. (Galatians 5:22-23)

I've lost my childhood fear of the Holy *Ghost* and have found, instead, that the presence of the Holy *Spirit* in my life is the good gift of my heavenly Father.

I hope you realize that **God loves you** and is actively involved in your life. Here's a simple explanation of how we know this.

Love comes from God

> Dear friends, let us love one another, for love comes from God. (1 John 4:7a)

CHAPTER 14

How Does God Act in My Life?

Many people think God is only interested in rules. But God is all about love. Jesus, God the Son, reminds us of the most important "rule":

> "'Love the Lord your God with all your heart and with all your soul and with all your mind.' This is the first and greatest commandment. And the second is like it: 'Love your neighbor as yourself.'" (Matthew 22:37-39)

"Okay," we say. "That sounds good." But we seem powerless to love like that.

Those who say, "I love God," and hate their brothers or sisters, are liars; for those who do not love a brother or sister whom they have seen, cannot love God whom they have not seen. The commandment we have from Him is this: those who love God must love their brothers and sisters also. (1 John 4:20-21 NRSV)

The power to love comes from God

Everyone who loves has been born of God and knows God. Whoever does not love does not know God, because God is love. This is how God showed His love among us: He sent His one and only Son into the world that we might live through Him. This is love: not that we loved God, but that He loved us and sent His Son as an atoning sacrifice for our sins. (1 John 4:7b-10)

Anything that we have done that is not loving separates us from a loving God. We don't have to murder or commit armed robbery to "sin." Sin is simply breaking God's commandment to love Him and others fully.

If we claim to be without sin, we deceive ourselves and the truth is not in us. (1 John 1:8)

But God's only Son, Jesus Christ, died and rose again to *atone* for our unloving behavior (1 John 2:1–2). Atone means to make *at one*. When we confess our lack of love (sin) and believe that Christ has died for our sin, we are forgiven and are *at one* with God and His love (see 1 John 1:9).

> If anyone acknowledges that Jesus is the Son of God, God lives in him and he in God. (1 John 4:15)

The power to love unselfishly comes from God

Love from God is not earned—it is a free gift—but it is *learned.*

> No one has ever seen God; but if we love one another, God lives in us and His love is made complete in us. (1 John 4:12)

We get to know God and His love better through reading His love letter (the Bible), talking to Him (prayer), and being with those who also love Him (the church). And the better we know God, the more we want to follow His commandment to love Him and others.

> This is love for God: to obey His commands. And His commands are not burdensome, for everyone born of God has overcome the world. (1 John 5:3-4a)

If you'd like more information about strengthening your faith relationship with God, talk to your minister or Christian youth leader. Or you can write me in care of the publisher (the address is in the introduction to **The Why Files** on page 12) or e-mail me at whyfiles@jameswatkins.com.

Maybe you're not a believer, and you're wondering what your Christian friends are talking about when they "testify" about being "**baptized**" or being "part of God's family." It all sounds pretty weird, doesn't it? And you're sure you don't want to be "slain in the Spirit" like you see on some TV evangelists' programs.

CHAPTER

15 What Does God Do to a Person?

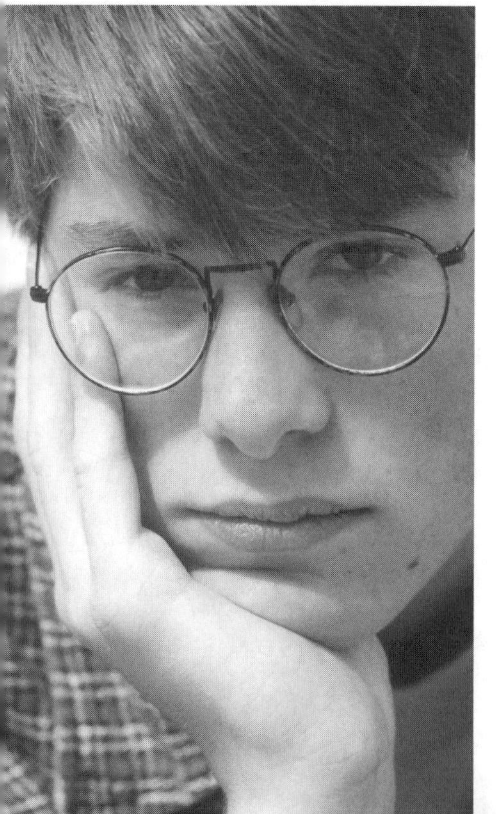

Or perhaps you attended an exciting youth conference or convention where you heard about salvation through Christ. There were probably a lot of tears and hugs and cheers as people celebrated their **faith**. But when you got off the bus, you may have found that those wonderful feelings had been left behind somewhere between the conference center and the church parking lot.

So what does God do in a believer's life?

Jesus tells a wonderful story that describes what God wants to do in each person's life.

Jesus continued: "There was a man who had two sons. The younger one said to his father, 'Father, give me my share of the estate.' So he divided his property between them.

"Not long after that, the younger son got together all he had, set off for a distant country and there squandered his wealth in wild living. After he had spent everything, there was a severe famine in that whole country, and he began to be in need. So he went and hired himself out to a citizen of that country, who sent him to his fields to feed pigs. He longed to fill his stomach with the pods that the pigs were eating, but no one gave him anything.

"When he came to his senses, he said, 'How many of my father's hired men have food to spare, and here I am starving to death! I will set out and go back to my father and say to him: Father, I have sinned against heaven and against you. I am no longer worthy to be called your son; make me like one of your hired men.' So he got up and went to his father.

"But while he was still a long way off, his father saw him and was filled with compassion for him; he ran to his son, threw his arms around him and kissed him.

"The son said to him, 'Father, I have sinned against heaven and against you. I am no longer worthy to be called your son.'

"But the father said to his servants, 'Quick! Bring the best robe and put it on him. Put a ring on his finger and sandals on his feet. Bring the fattened calf and kill it. Let's have a feast and celebrate. For this son of mine was dead and is alive again; he was lost and is found.' So they began to celebrate." (Luke 15:11-24)

Have you ever felt like the prodigal son (or daughter)? I have! I thought I knew what would bring me joy and satisfaction. If I could just be a famous author, I'd be satisfied.

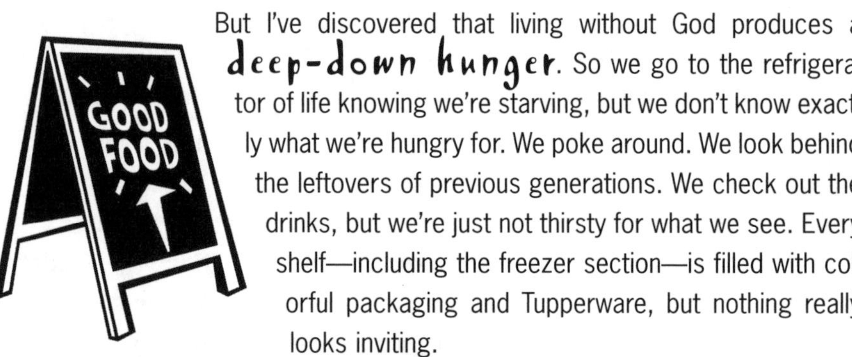

But I've discovered that living without God produces a **deep-down hunger**. So we go to the refrigerator of life knowing we're starving, but we don't know exactly what we're hungry for. We poke around. We look behind the leftovers of previous generations. We check out the drinks, but we're just not thirsty for what we see. Every shelf—including the freezer section—is filled with colorful packaging and Tupperware, but nothing really looks inviting.

Have you ever felt that way—**starving**, but you don't know what you're hungry for? I think that's the main reason young people and adults are turning to the New Age, witchcraft, psychics, and cults. In junior high, I can remember feeling as though I were spiritually starving to death. That's because each of us is created with what Augustine, an early church leader, described as a God-shaped vacuum.

But when we wander away from Him, God doesn't leave us in the pigpen with an empty stomach.

> For God so loved the world that He gave His one and only Son, that whoever believes in Him shall not perish but have eternal life. (John 3:16)

> You see, at just the right time, when we were still powerless, Christ died for the ungodly. Very rarely will anyone die for a righteous man, though for a good man someone might possibly dare to die. But God demonstrates His own love for us in this: While we were still sinners, Christ died for us. (Romans 5:6–8)

Before we even know what's happening, God the Holy Spirit makes us aware of that hunger. Maybe it's through Christians who share their faith and seem to have something that we don't have. Perhaps it's through reading God's Word or going to church or a Bible study with a friend.

Like a parent standing at the front door waiting for a child to return, God is waiting for us. And better than just waiting at the door, He sends His Holy Spirit to work faith in Christ in our hearts and bring us home to Him.

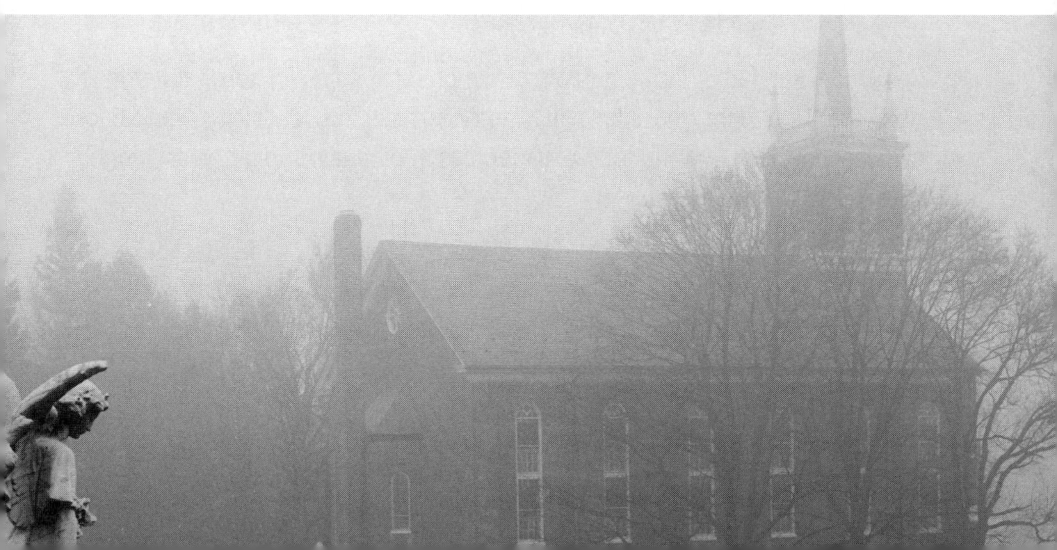

How can God forgive me when I've done so many bad things?

God Forgives Us

No matter how badly we've rebelled or simply ignored God, He **welcomes** us home.

> If we confess our sins, He is faithful and just and will forgive us our sins and purify us from all unrighteousness. (1 John 1:9)

> "Repent and be baptized, every one of you, in the name of Jesus Christ for the forgiveness of your sins. And you will receive the gift of the Holy Spirit." (Acts 2:38)

> Therefore, since we have been justified through faith, we have peace with God through our Lord Jesus Christ. (Romans 5:1)

God doesn't just welcome us back, He provides the person to bring us back—Jesus Christ. Through Jesus' death, all our sins are washed away and we stand before God clothed in Christ's perfection.

Remember the father in the parable of the prodigal son? Notice what he does. He yells, "How dare you spend the family fortune! You're going to pay back every penny if you want to live under this roof again, young man!" Right? WRONG!

> "But while he was still a long way off, his father saw him and was filled with compassion for him; he ran to his son, threw his arms around him and kissed him." (Luke 15:20)

Why did Jesus die on the cross for everyone—even those who rejected Him?

That's *grace*—undeserved love and acceptance. The prodigal son didn't deserve a royal welcome, but "the father said to his servants, 'Quick! Bring the best robe and put it on him. Put a ring on his finger and sandals on his feet. Bring the fattened calf and kill it. Let's have a feast and celebrate'" (Luke 5:22–23).

Paul writes about this kind of forgiveness and grace:

> "We believe it is through the grace of our Lord Jesus that we are saved, just as they are." (Acts 15:11b)
>
> For all have sinned and fall short of the glory of God, and are justified freely by His grace through the redemption that came by Christ Jesus. (Romans 3:23-24)
>
> For it is by grace you have been saved, through faith—and this not from yourselves, it is the gift of God—not by works, so that no one can boast. (Ephesians 2:8-9)

God Justifies Us

The theological term for being forgiven by God is to be justified. God declares sinners to be righteous, or without sin, because of Christ's saving work for us. Our sins were put on Christ, and He carried out our death sentence. He gives us the righteousness He earned for us on the cross. When we confess our faith in Jesus Christ and are baptized, our "criminal record" is completely erased.

If Jesus had continued the story of the prodigal son's return, we'd never, ever hear the father bring up the son's squandering of the family fortune.

God Reconciles Us to Himself

Another part of this forgiveness is *reconciliation.*

> Since we have now been justified by His blood, how much more shall we be saved from God's wrath through Him! For if, when we were God's enemies, we were reconciled to Him through the death of His Son, how much more, having been reconciled, shall we be saved through His life! Not only is this so, but we also rejoice in God through our Lord Jesus Christ, through whom we have now received reconciliation. (Roman 5:9-11)

You've probably heard of *reconciliation* in terms of marriage or race relations. Two people or groups are separated by hate or distrust, but through reconciliation they are reunited. The father in the story could have forgiven his son, but then could have been cold and distant. "I forgive you, but we can never have a close relationship again after what you did." But the father didn't react this way. He loved his son and his forgiveness included reinstatement into the life of the family as a precious son.

> Once you were alienated from God and were enemies in your minds because of your evil behavior. But now He has reconciled you by Christ's physical body through death to present you holy in His sight, without blemish and free from accusation. (Colossians 1:21-22)

God Adopts Us as His Children

In first-century culture, putting a ring on someone's finger didn't mean you were going steady. The signet ring, with a raised ID symbol, was the MasterCard of the first century. So if you had Dad's ring, you had everything you needed as a child. (Would you give your kid your credit cards if he had just spent his entire inheritance on wine and wild women?! God's grace is not only "amazing," it's **outrageous!**)

> Those who are led by the Spirit of God are sons [and daughters] of God. For you did not receive a spirit that makes you a slave again to fear, but you received the Spirit of sonship [daughtership]. And by Him we cry, "Abba, Father." The Spirit Himself testifies with our spirit that we are God's children. Now if we are children, then we are heirs—heirs of God and co-heirs with Christ. (Romans 8:14-17)

For some of you, the concept of God as a father is not a comforting thought. Steve had been rejected and abused by his earthly father, so I wasn't surprised when he nearly shouted at a Bible study, "If God is my Father, I hate His guts." Perhaps thinking of God as the parent you've always wanted and needed is more helpful than comparing Him to an imperfect earthly parent.

God Makes Us a New Creation

But God doesn't simply forgive us: "Therefore, if anyone is in Christ, he is a new creation; the old has gone, the new has come!" (2 Corinthians 5:17).

Buck restores old cars. “Wow! It looks like it just rolled off the assembly line—50 years ago!” I said in amazement at his 1941 Ford sedan. Like a proud parent, Buck showed me pictures of what the glistening white car had looked like before five years of pounding out dents, rebuilding fenders, and completely reupholstering the interior. The “lizzie” is now more fiberglass than “tin,” but it looks factory fresh.

Christ, however, doesn’t rebuild, reconstruct, rehabilitate, rejuvenate, replace, or even restore. **He recreates!** No filled-in dents. No cover-ups. No cosmetic paint jobs. He gives us forgiveness and the Holy Spirit to enable us to live new lives to His glory.

God Works in the Lives of His Children

Paul writes to his Christian friends:

> Therefore, I urge you, brothers, in view of God’s mercy, to offer your bodies as living sacrifices, holy and pleasing to God—this is your spiritual act of worship. Do not conform any longer to the pattern of this world, but be transformed by the renewing of your mind. Then you will be able to test and approve what God’s will is—His good, pleasing and perfect will. (Romans 12:1-2)

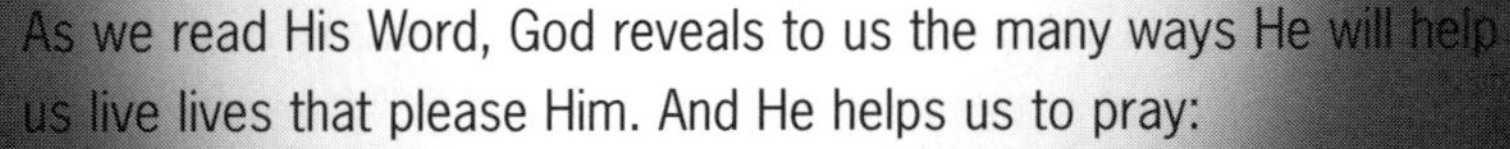

As we read His Word, God reveals to us the many ways He will help us live lives that please Him. And He helps us to pray:

"Jesus, I need Your help in getting along with my kid brother."
"Father, please help me love my phys. ed. teacher!"
"Holy Spirit, I need Your help with my thought life."

Maybe you're struggling with such an area of your life. Don't get discouraged! Read again that last sentence of Romans 12:2. God will help you **test the choices** you face and point you into the paths He wants you to take.

Even as God asks us to be "living sacrifices" and tells us not to "conform any longer to the pattern of this world" (or as J. B. Phillips paraphrases it, "Don't let the world squeeze you into its mold"), He knows we will fail. But He promises to forgive our sins for Jesus' sake. By the power of the Holy Spirit working through the Word and the sacraments, we will

> Put to death, therefore, whatever belongs to your earthly nature: sexual immorality, impurity, lust, evil desires and greed,

> which is idolatry. ... But now you must rid yourselves of all such things as these: anger, rage, malice, slander, and filthy language from your lips. (Colossians 3:5, 8)

The Holy Spirit keeps us from falling into the same old way of thinking and acting. Because He is active in our lives, we exhibit the **"fruit of the Spirit"**: love, joy, peace, patience, kindness, goodness, faithfulness, gentleness, and self-control (Galatians 5:22–23).

In Romans 6:11–14, Paul writes:

> In the same way, count yourselves dead to sin but alive to God in Christ Jesus. Therefore do not let sin reign in your mortal body so that you obey its evil desires. Do not offer the parts of your body to sin, as instruments of wickedness, but rather offer yourselves to God, as those who have been brought from death to life; and offer the parts of your body to Him as instruments of righteousness. For sin shall not be your master.

Why is God so judgmental?

Wow! We just read that God loves us unconditionally, then the Bible sounds so judgmental about sin! Look back at chapter 10. Remember that among God's attributes or characteristics are righteousness and holiness. One way that God's hatred of sin is seen in our lives is in the way He acts in our lives as our *heavenly Father*. Just like an earthly father protects his kids, God protects us from those things that will hurt us. That's one reason He has given us the Ten Commandments.

Because I love my children, I'm intolerant and judgmental when it comes to Faith and Paul. If I really love my daughter and son, I'm going to be narrow-minded toward anything that is harmful to their physical, mental, social, and spiritual well-being. That's why I'm judgmental toward plaque build-up, kiddy porn, gangs, strep throat, put-downs, undercooked hamburgers, spaced-out cults, illegal drugs, and tobacco executives who are simply serial killers in suits.

And if I'm that protective of my two kids, think how God feels about all of us! There are a few more words at the end of that section in Romans 6. It doesn't end with "for sin shall not be your master," but continues with "because you are not under law, but under grace."

The apostle Paul thought of sin as a power that enslaves, so to make his point, he calls it a "master." Before you start thinking that living under grace means you can go wild with sinning because you're not bound by the law anymore, hold on. What Paul means is that the law, as it was understood in Old Testament times, doesn't give the sinner any power to resist sin; it only condemns him when he does sin. But grace, on the other hand, enables. Because we have **GOD'S GRACE**, we have His Holy Spirit to guide our thoughts and actions into those things that please God.

Do you still feel that you're just too bad for God to work in your life? Check out the believers in the First Church of Corinth who had once been ...

> ... sexually immoral ... idolaters ... adulterers ... male prostitutes ... homosexual offenders ... thieves ... the greedy ... drunkards ... slanderers ... swindlers. ... But you were washed, you were sanctified, you were justified in the name of the Lord Jesus Christ and by the Spirit of our God. (1 Corinthians 6:9-11)

That's exactly what God loves to do: take people who once hated Him and broke every one of His commandments and

justify,

reconcile,

adopt

and transform them through

Jesus Christ!

"I can't see where we're going!" Headlights of oncoming cars **blurred** into an eerie glow as Dave cautiously inched off the road.

"I'll scrape it off," I offered, venturing into the freezing rain and slush. But three blocks later, the windshield was once again iced over. I went back into the storm for more scraping and shivering.

CHAPTER 16

How Do You Know When God Is Talking to You?

During the moments the '67 Volkswagen was actually moving, Dave and I reviewed the Bible study about hearing God's voice that we had just attended.

How can you hear God?

"I know the frustration you were talking about, Dave. I remember my third-grade Sunday school teacher telling the story of Moses and the burning bush. I spent the whole afternoon sitting on the back steps waiting for the spirea bush to burst into flames and this booming voice to say, 'James Norman Watkins! Yea and verily, I sayeth unto thee, take off thy sneakers for thou art standing on hallowed ground.'

Nothing! The next week, she told the story of God speaking to the entire Hebrew nation from the smoke and fire of Mt. Sinai. So I spent one night staring into our trash burner, but the only thing I got was sick from smoke inhalation."

"Jim, you're really weird."

When I ask for guidance from God, why don't I receive it?

"You're probably right. But the most frustrating thing is hearing older Christians say, 'God spoke to me about—whatever.' I've knelt by my bed, tried to quiet my mind, and prayed, 'God, I'm trying to figure out if this thing is right or wrong. PLEASE tell me.'"

"And absolutely nothing happens, right?"

"Right! You have the same problem?"

By this time, the windshield was coated once more.

"Hey, Dave, it's actually starting to **defrost** a spot on my side!" I moved some gloves, a 10-year-old road map, and a paperback book to see through the clear area. "Tell you what. You run the gas and the brakes from your side, and I'll steer from over here."

"Well, I guess it's that or spend the rest of our lives on Capital Avenue. Tell me when we come to red lights and curves and pedestrians and stuff."

What is God's will for my life?

Obviously we arrived home alive or there would be another person's name on the cover of this book. But lying in bed that night, my mind floated from our questions about "hearing God" to our daring ride in the sleet. We had been searching for signs, fleeces, omens, visions, or dreams that would give us some indication of God's thoughts on various issues and decisions we both faced. (Everything from "What sophomore classes should I take next semester?" to "Who am I going to marry?")

The blinding sleet seemed to be a meaningful metaphor of our inability to see down the road of life. But maybe that was also the answer!

1. God is at the "steering wheel" of your life.

St. Paul writes:

> Therefore, I urge you, brothers, in view of God's mercy, to offer your bodies as living sacrifices, holy and pleasing to God—this is your spiritual act of worship. Do not conform any longer to the pattern of this world, but be transformed by the renewing of your mind. Then you will be able to test and approve what God's will is—His good, pleasing and perfect will. (Romans 12:1-2)

I had not fully trusted God to direct my life. I had been driving blindly down the road of life, when God wanted to give me meaning and purpose in my journey. He was in the car, but I didn't trust His steering.

You can't trust someone you don't know, as Chuck and I discovered one night in high school. My friend had borrowed his parents' brand new T-bird, we'd splashed on half a bottle of aftershave and headed for the big game to meet some girls. As we approached a traffic light, a car that looked like something Fred Flintstone had traded in seemed stalled in the intersection. We swung around the car, squealed our tires, and roared down the street.

Suddenly, "Fred" began gaining on us, then pulled beside us. His face was scarred, and his eyes glared out of the deep sockets. "Let's lose this psycho!" I shouted.

Chuck stomped the accelerator. But the faster we sped, the faster Fred sped to keep alongside us. Out of the corner of my eye, I saw him reach for something chrome-plated.

"He's got a gun, Chuck!" I tried to pull my friend onto the floorboard with me as he tried to regain control of the *speeding* car. Then our worst fears were realized. It was a badge! It was a member of our Battle Creek Township Police undercover unit.

That was my second experience with the BCTP. One bright summer day, my brother and I decided to let our guinea pigs see the world outside their cages. Hamlette and Squeaky were munching on grass and enjoying their newfound freedom. Suddenly, both spied a hole in the base of our cement block garage! Within seconds, our **guinea pigs** had vanished into the concrete hideout.

So what does a mom do when her 5- and 8-year-olds are crying hysterically and two guinea pigs are holed up in their bunker? She calls the Battle Creek Township Police. As a second-grader, I thought that black and white car was the most beautiful sight I had ever seen. I knew The Lone Ranger and Tonto had arrived to save our pets from certain death.

Why is following God's will so scary?

What was the difference between my two reactions to the local law officers? In one case, I knew help had arrived. In the second, I knew Chuck and I were in big trouble—**BIG** trouble.

I felt the same way about God. I could see Him looking at me from the driver's seat, and I just knew that the only way I would be a writer was if I grabbed the wheel. After all, wouldn't God expect me to prove my commitment to Him by torching my typewriter?

Then I discovered Romans 12:2. God's will is "good, pleasing and perfect"! I began to get to know God. I discovered He wanted the steering wheel not to manipulate or enslave me, but to give me meaningful direction. It wasn't until I read about—and believed in—His *unconditional love* that I trusted Him to provide direction for my life.

2. Trust the Driver.

When God is at the wheel, we can trust Him to direct us along the best routes. Just as I had to clear away the clutter from the dashboard to be able to see the road, God clears away the **clutter** in our lives to help us better see the roads on which He is driving us.

Again in Romans 12, Paul urges us: "Do not conform any longer to the pattern of this world, but be transformed by the renewing of your mind. *Then* you will be able to test and approve what God's will is—His good, pleasing and perfect will (Romans 12:2, italics mine).

Disobeying God breaks our communication line with Him. When the Holy Spirit guides our thoughts and actions, we see God's plan for our lives.

3. Look to the Light.

Dave paid close attention to my shouts of "Red light!" "Down shift for this curve!" and "Okay, the light's green." But how do we "hear" God? How do we "see" the paths He would have us take? God speaks through Scripture. All we need to know about "God's will"—what He loves, what He hates, what's important to Him—is found in His Word. And in this Word, we are continually pointed to the only Light of the world—Jesus Christ—who came so we would never have to live in darkness or fear again.

Your word is a lamp to my feet and a light to my path. … The unfolding of Your words gives light. (Psalm 119:105, 130a)

In Him [Jesus] was life, and that life was the light of men. (John 1:4)

[Jesus said,] “I am the light of the world. Whoever follows Me will never walk in darkness, but will have the light of life.”(John 8:12).

For God, who said, “Let light shine out of darkness,” made His light shine in our hearts to give us the light of the knowledge of the glory of God in the face of Christ. (2 Corinthians 4:6)

You are all sons [and daughers] of light and … of the day. (1 Thessalonians 5:5)

As sons and daughters of God, we trust that He is at the wheel. While we'll have a few bumps and “S” curves in the road of life, “He will direct our paths” until we safely pull up to the Pearly Gates.

From the newsroom ...

More than 8,000 pilgrims visit Mario Rubio's small stucco house in rural New Mexico to see skillet burns on a tortilla resembling the mournful face of Jesus.

TV evangelist and faith healer Oral Roberts is told by a 900-foot Jesus to raise $8,000,000 for his hospital complex—or die!

CHAPTER 17

What about Visions and Miracles and Things Like That?

Jesus appears in Fostoria, Ohio, on the side of a soybean oil tank. Skeptics suggest it's only rust.

Jesus also appears on the chimney of the Town and Country bowling alley in suburban Chicago. All agree the four-foot-high image is formed from rusting metal, but locals are split on whether it's Jesus or Popeye.

Jesus makes national news when He appears in the strands of spaghetti on 35 Pizza Hut billboards in Atlanta.

Appearances by Mary, the mother of Jesus, also have been reported since medieval times in Europe and more recently in the New World. Visions, as well as weeping and bleeding statues of Mary, also have been reported. In a few cases, the site of the appearance becomes a permanent **shrine**, such as Lourdes, where believers come to pray for healing.

So are these visions and visitations actually, well, visions and visitations?

Visions and Dreams

The Bible does describe visions, visitations, dreams, miracles, signs, and wonders.

> In the year that King Uzziah died, I saw the Lord seated on a throne, high and exalted, and the train of His robe filled the temple. Above Him were seraphs, each with six wings: With two wings they covered their faces, with two they covered their feet, and with two they were flying. And they were calling to one another: "Holy, holy, holy is the LORD Almighty; the whole earth is full of His glory." At the sound of their voices the doorposts and thresholds shook and the temple was filled with smoke. (Isaiah 6:1-4)

> I looked up and there before me was a man dressed in linen, with a belt of the finest gold around his waist. His body was like chrysolite, his face like lightning, his eyes like flaming torches, his arms and legs like the gleam of burnished bronze, and his voice like the sound of a multitude. I, Daniel, was the only one who saw the vision; the men with

me did not see it, but such terror overwhelmed them that they fled and hid themselves. So I was left alone, gazing at this great vision; I had no strength left, my face turned deathly pale and I was helpless. (Daniel 10:5-8)

This is how the birth of Jesus Christ came about: His mother Mary was pledged to be married to Joseph, but before they came together, she was found to be with child through the Holy Spirit. Because Joseph her husband was a righteous man and did not want to expose her to public disgrace, he had in mind to divorce her quietly. But after he had considered this, an angel of the Lord appeared to him in a dream and said, "Joseph son of David, do not be afraid to take Mary home as your wife, because what is conceived in her is from the Holy Spirit. She will give birth to a son, and you are to give Him the name Jesus, because He will save His people from their sins." (Matthew 1:18-21)

As he neared Damascus on his journey, suddenly a light from heaven flashed around him. He fell to the ground and heard a voice say to him, "Saul, Saul, why do you persecute Me?" "Who are You, Lord?" Saul asked. "I am Jesus, whom you are persecuting," He replied. "Now get up and go into the city, and you will be told what you must do." The men traveling with Saul stood there speechless; they heard the sound but did not see anyone. (Acts 9:3-7)

Signs and Miracles

Unfortunately, the word **miracle** has been used to describe everything from giving birth to a healthy newborn to winning the Readers' Digest Sweepstakes. Norman Geisler defines a miracle as a

> ***... divine intervention into, or interruption of, the regular course of the world that produces a purposeful but unusual event that would not have occurred otherwise.***[34]

As we shared in the chapter about the Trinity, miracles are beyond our ability to comprehend because there is no known natural cause. The miracle may not be contrary to natural laws but simply above and beyond them. For instance, archaeologists discovered natural gas under the remains of Sodom and Gomorrah, which were divinely destroyed by God. Perhaps He simply triggered a huge explosion at the exact moment Lot and his family were safely out of town. (The natural gas deposits are *natural*. The precise location and timing of any explosion are not.)

In Scripture, we see three periods of what I'd call "mega" miracles.

In Exodus we find the **plagues**, the Red Sea opening up, the walls of Jericho crashing down, the sun standing still, etc. Definitely the "mega" variety! Then for several centuries, no miracles were reported.

During the time of the prophets, we see another set of miracles with Elijah calling down *fire from heaven* on the altar of Baal and the fiery

chariot that takes Elijah from this earth. Then, for more than 400 years, God appeared to be silent.

The third period is during the ministry of Christ. He raises the dead, heals the sick, calms stormy seas, feeds 5,000 hungry men with a boy's lunch, and then—the grand finale—**rises from the dead** Himself. (We'll talk specifically about healings in the next chapter.)

The apostle John, who had the vision that gave us the book of the Revelation, sums up the purpose for miracles:

> Jesus did many other miraculous signs in the presence of His disciples, which are not recorded in this book. But these are written that you may believe that Jesus is the Christ, the Son of God, and that by believing you may have life in His name. (John 20:30-31)

The miracles recorded in the Bible are specifically designed to show God and His power to His creation. Many commentators believe the "mega" miracles ceased in the first century because God now reveals Himself through His written Word, the Bible. We no longer need visions and **signs from heaven** to communicate God's truth.

So what about visions and miracles today?

First, Jesus warns us not to seek visions and signs.

> Then some of the Pharisees and teachers of the law said to Him, "Teacher, we want to see a miraculous sign from You." He answered, "A wicked and adulterous generation asks for a miraculous sign!" (Matthew 12:38-39)

Second, Jesus tells Thomas, who had initially refused to believe He was resurrected, "Because you have seen Me, you have believed; blessed are those who have not seen and yet have believed" (John 20:29).

Obviously, God is God and can perform miracles as well as appear in visions anytime He wants. And at the end of time, God will once again perform the miracles we read about in the book of Revelation. But for now, I would be very skeptical of a 900-foot Jesus or "Our Lord of the Soybean Oil Storage Tank." Likewise, the Roman Catholic Church has actively and consistently refused to recognize the **authenticity** of most visions of Mary. It has recognized a small number of healings as "miraculous," but rejected the vast majority of claims as unfounded.

At the same time, I have no doubts that those who see these apparitions are sincere. But as we talked about in the self-fulfilling prophecies of psychics, people who see visions of Jesus may be convincing themselves that is what they've seen. For instance, if you carefully evaluate contemporary sightings of Mary, you'll notice that the person initially reports only having seen "a figure" or "a lady." The idea that the object seen is Mary is an interpretation added to the story by friends and relatives. The person is talked into believing, by herself or others, that Mary will appear to her at the site of the original vision and will have "messages" for her. The person seeing the vision is almost always in a difficult situation financially or politically and is desperate for a "sign" from God that He has not forgotten her.

Unfortunately, visions, dreams, signs, wonders, and the like don't always **strengthen** faith in God. Only a short time after God parted the Red Sea for His people to escape the Egyptian army, the Israelites built an idol to one of the Egyptian gods. As soon as Jesus raised Lazarus from the dead—which ought to be proof enough that He is God—the religious rulers plotted to kill both Jesus and Lazarus.

And because God has a greater plan than our health and wealth, He often chooses not to miraculously bail us out of trouble.

God closed the mouths of the lions for Daniel, but hundreds of early Christians were killed by the big cats as Roman "entertainment." Shadrach, Meshach, and Abednego survived being thrown into Nebuchadnezzar's fiery furnace, but hundreds of Christians were used by Nero as human patio torches. Peter was miraculously rescued from prison, but just a few verses earlier, James was beheaded.

Hebrews 11, the "faith chapter," recalls incredible stories of God's miracle-working power. But it ends this way:

And what more shall I say? I do not have time to tell about Gideon, Barak, Samson, Jephthah, David, Samuel and the prophets, who through faith conquered kingdoms, administered justice, and gained what was promised; who shut the mouths of lions, quenched the fury of the flames, and escaped the edge of the sword; whose weakness was turned to strength; and who became powerful in battle and routed foreign armies. Women received back their dead, raised to life again. Others were tortured and refused to be released, so that they might gain a better resurrection.

> Some faced jeers and flogging, while still others were chained and put in prison. They were stoned; they were sawed in two; they were put to death by the sword. They went about in sheepskins and goatskins, destitute, persecuted and mistreated—the world was not worthy of them. They wandered in deserts and mountains, and in caves and holes in the ground. These were all commended for their faith, yet none of them received what had been promised. (Hebrews 11:32-39)

Yes, it's exciting to hear stories about modern-day signs and wonders! But that's not always God's plan. He invites us to believe in Jesus through His Word, the Bible, not burned tortilla shells.

"Monica" begins to glow as she announces, "I am an angel sent by God." The angels on the TV drama *Touched by an Angel* don't have **wings or halos** and that's an executive decision. When Martha Williamson was approached by the CBS suits to be producer of the popular show, she agreed to the project only if she could present what she believed:

CHAPTER 18

Are There Really Angels?

1. That angels are messengers of God, not ends in themselves.
2. That angels aren't fairies flapping their wings and granting wishes.
3. That God is someone to reckon with.
4. That at the end of each show the angels do not win—God does.

She also stipulated, no deceased humans needing a few more good deeds to get to heaven and no deity portrayed as an old man with a beard.[35]

Bible scholars may not agree on each point of the Hollywood scriptwriter's theology. However, *Touched by an Angel* is far closer to Scripture than the foul-mouthed, womanizing *Michael,* who movie posters described as "an angel, not a saint."

The Bible includes more than **300** references to angels, so how do heavenly angels differ from the Hollywood variety?

Where did angels come from?
When we die, do we become angels?

Angels Are Created Beings

Angels are not departed humans with wings and supernatural powers. (Sorry, fans of *It's a Wonderful Life* with the lovable, bumbling angel, Clarence, or Michael Landon's heart-tugging *Highway to Heaven.*) The Bible states:

> Praise the LORD. Praise the LORD from the heavens, praise Him in the heights above. Praise Him, all His angels, praise Him, all His heavenly hosts. ... Let them praise the name of the LORD, for He commanded and they were created. (Psalm 148:1-2, 5)
>
> For by [Christ] all things were created: things in heaven and on earth, visible and invisible, whether thrones or powers or rulers or authorities; all things were created by Him and for Him. (Colossians 1:16)

Do angels have separate sexes?

And, contrary to John Travolta's *Michael* and Nicholas Cage's portrayal in *City of Angels*, angels are **genderless** and don't marry (Luke 20:34–36). So we can assume they don't lust after earthly women, either.

What do angels look like?

Angels Are Fearsome-Looking Creatures

One of the most popular images of angels in gift shops has those two fat cherubs with wings staring reflectively off into the heavens. Cherubim, however, are described in Scripture just a bit differently.

> Their faces looked like this: Each of the four had the face of a man, and on the right side each had the face of a lion, and on the left the face of an ox; each also had the face of an eagle. Such were their faces. Their wings were spread out upward; each had two wings, one touching the wing of another creature on either side, and two wings covering its body. Each one went straight ahead. Wherever the spirit would

> go, they would go, without turning as they went. The appearance of the living creatures was like burning coals of fire or like torches. Fire moved back and forth among the creatures; it was bright, and lightning flashed out of it. The creatures sped back and forth like flashes of lightning. (Ezekiel 1:10–14)

These scary-looking cherubim were placed at the entrance of the Garden of Eden to prevent Adam and Eve from reentering.

Isaiah came face to face with another variety of angels: *seraphs*.

> Above Him were seraphs, each with six wings: With two wings they covered their faces, with two they covered their feet, and with two they were flying. And they were calling to one another: "Holy, holy, holy is the LORD Almighty; the whole earth is full of His glory." At the sound of their voices the doorposts and thresholds shook and the temple was filled with smoke. (Isaiah 6:2–4)

Can angels appear as humans?

At other times, however, angels took on the form of flesh and blood, as in the cases of visitors to Lot, the parents of Samson, Mary, the shepherds, the women at Jesus' tomb, and those who were present at Christ's ascension.

Are there angels in heaven with God?

Angels Were Created to Worship God

Angels were created **pure and holy** to worship God in His very presence.

> All the angels were standing around the throne and around the elders and the four living creatures. They fell down on their faces before the throne and worshiped God, saying: "Amen! Praise and glory and wisdom and thanks and honor and power and strength be to our God for ever and ever. Amen!" (Revelation 7:11-12)

Why were demons created?

God didn't create demons. Bible scholars believe one-third of these angels "did not keep their positions of authority but abandoned their own home" (Jude 6) in a rebellion, apparently led by Satan. These **fallen angels**—or demons—oppose God's work (Daniel 10:12–13),[36] inflict disease (Luke 13:16), tempt people to sin (Matthew 4:3), and spread false doctrine (1 Timothy 4:1). But this was not God's intention for heavenly beings. (We'll talk more about Satan and demons in the next chapter.)

Angels Were Created to Serve God and His Creation

Hebrews 1:14 asks, "Are not all angels ministering spirits sent to serve those who will inherit salvation?"

God sent a trio of angels to warn Lot and his family of the impending destruction of Sodom and Gomorrah (Genesis 19). He also sent an angel to close the lions' mouths when Daniel was thrown to the beasts (Daniel 6). Angels told Mary (Luke 1:26–38) and Joseph (Matthew 1:20–21) about the miraculous conception of Jesus. An angel also warned Joseph to flee to Egypt with Mary and Jesus to avoid Herod's jealous massacre of Bethlehem's babies (Matthew 2:13).

We find angels ministering to Jesus in the desert following His temptation (Matthew 4); with Him as He prayed in the Garden of Gethsemane (Luke 22:43); announcing His resurrection (Luke 24:1–8); and appearing to His followers when Jesus returned to heaven (Acts 1:11).

Angels also sprang Peter from jail (Acts 12) and encouraged Paul while he was ministering in Corinth (Acts 27:23–24).

We can imply from various stories of angelic interventions that angels do offer direction and protection to God's people, but not as fairy godmothers that grant our wishes. Angels are God's servants, not ours.

And we shouldn't assume that angels are always friends of humans. Contrary to the dapper angel of death, Andrew, on *Touched by an Angel,* the Bible's "angel of the LORD" killed 185,000 Assyrians who had threatened to invade Jerusalem (2 Kings 19:35). According to Acts 12:23, another angel killed the boasting King Herod mid-sentence.

The book of Revelation teaches that angels will execute God's judgment upon a rebellious world:

> The first angel went and poured out his bowl on the land, and ugly and painful sores broke out on the people who had the mark of the beast and worshiped his image.
>
> The second angel poured out his bowl on the sea,

and it turned into blood like that of a dead man, and every living thing in the sea died.

The third angel poured out his bowl on the rivers and springs of water, and they became blood. …

The fourth angel poured out his bowl on the sun, and the sun was given power to scorch people with fire. They were seared by the intense heat and they cursed the name of God, who had control over these plagues, but they refused to repent and glorify Him.

The fifth angel poured out his bowl on the throne of the beast, and his kingdom was plunged into darkness. Men gnawed their tongues in agony and cursed the God of heaven because of their pains and their sores, but they refused to repent of what they had done.

The sixth angel poured out his bowl on the great river Euphrates, and its water was dried up to prepare the way for the kings from the East. …

The seventh angel poured out his bowl into the air, and out of the temple came a loud voice from the throne, saying, “It is done!”

Then there came flashes of lightning, rumblings, peals of thunder and a severe earthquake. No earthquake like it has ever occurred since man has been on earth, so tremendous was the quake. (Revelation 16:2-4, 8-12, 17-18)

Angels Are All Around

Touched by an Angel certainly doesn't have the budget to cast all of God's angels. The apostle John describes a scene of "angels, numbering thousands upon thousands, and ten thousand times ten thousand" (Revelation 5:11).

Do we really have guardian angels?

The ancient Talmud, a Jewish book of religious law, claims every Hebrew had 11,000 guardian angels. Later, Martin Luther calculated the angel population at **10 trillion**—enough for more than one thousand for every person—Jew and Gentile—on earth.

We may never see with earthly eyes these heavenly beings or know the many ways they have protected and guided, but they are real. They are active. And they are, as the producer of TV angels warns, "messengers of God, not ends in themselves."

"My mom's completely flipped out. I mean, she sees demons everywhere. Just this morning, the car died on the way to school. She got out, pounded on the hood, and yelled, 'In the name of Jesus, I command the foul spirits of engine stalling to come OUT!' "

Tina* was one teen I could always count on to be in church and youth meetings. She shifted in

CHAPTER 19

Are There Really "Fallen" Angels Like the Devil and Demons?

the office chair and twisted a strand of her blond hair. "It's really weird. She threw out my Oxy-10 and tried to cast out the demons of **clogged pores**. Now she's convinced that my room's a wreck because I have an 'unclean spirit.'"

Tina stared out the window as she tried to sort it all out. "Mom's acting really weird. But after last week, I know that Satan and demons are real."

* Not her real name

That week, Tina, her friend Karen, and two guys from the youth group, Kevin and John, had been at our house playing Uno when the phone rang.

"Jim, Bret's growling and snarling like a wild animal and trying to jump off the balcony! He keeps saying that Satan's coming for him," a concerned voice said.

I yelled for Kevin and John to come with me and asked Tina, Karen, and my wife to pray for Bret—and for us.

When we arrived, Bret was thrashing around on the **second-story balcony** with two other guys from the youth group sitting on his chest.

"Stay away from me or I'll kill you!" Bret screamed. I decided that might be good advice.

"Do you know if he's taken anything like PCP or speed?" I asked.

"No, he's been here all night!" Roy yelled from the balcony. "He was okay until we started talking about Jesus." Bret showed up at church for videos and pizza, but he always seemed to avoid the Bible studies. I cautiously began climbing the stairs.

Can demons physically harm you?

"I told you I'd kill you! He's mine!" The **screeching** voice sounded nothing like Bret's—it reverberated with a raspy, hollow sound. The August air hung hot and heavy, but I instantly felt chilled, and my body began to shake. Still suspicious that he was on something, I sniffed the air. I nearly gagged on the rotten-egg smell of sulfur.

"In the name of Jesus Christ and by the power of His blood, I command you to come out of Bret." The words coming out of my mouth surprised me, as if someone else had voiced them. I was even more amazed when Bret instantly relaxed and stared at the two young men sitting on his chest as he lay sprawled on the balcony.

"What's happening? What are you doing here ..." Bret completed the sentence by sneering "Christian" in a threatening voice, his eyes **burning** straight through me. He tossed his two friends against the house with no apparent effort. "I told you that you can't have Bret. If we can't have him, neither can you." Bret bolted for the edge of the balcony as all five of us pounced on him.

For more than an hour, we struggled with Bret, prayed, and pleaded for **Christ's power** over the evil that seemed to possess Bret. Finally, Bret asked Christ to come to his aid, and the attacks ceased.

Can demons really possess your body?

Now, sitting with Tina only one week later, I couldn't explain away satanic manifestations as merely primitive superstition or mental disorder. Something—or someone—had been controlling Bret.

What do demons look like?

As we discussed in the chapter about angels, demons are fallen angels, so I would assume they have the same characteristics as angels—namely, they are spiritual beings.

Some theologians believe Ezekiel describes Satan's fall from grace. (Others believe this passage is referring only to an earthly king.)

> "'This is what the Sovereign LORD says: "You were the model of perfection, full of wisdom and perfect in beauty. You were in Eden, the garden of God; every precious stone adorned you: ruby, topaz and emerald, chrysolite, onyx and jasper, sapphire, turquoise and beryl. Your settings and mountings were made of gold; on the day you were created they were prepared. You were anointed as a guardian cherub, for so I ordained you. You were on the holy mount of God; you walked among the fiery stones. You were blameless in your ways from the day you were created till wickedness was found in you. Through your widespread trade you were filled with violence, and you sinned. So I drove you in disgrace from the mount of God, and I expelled you, O guardian cherub, from among the fiery stones. Your heart became proud on account of your beauty, and you corrupted your wisdom because of your splendor."'" (Ezekiel 28:12b-17a)

So while God has created angels to "minister" to humans, Satan and his demons oppose everything that is godly and beneficial to people.

Should a Christian be afraid of demons?

I've got to admit the incident with Bret terrified me! But at the same time, there was an assurance that God was far greater than any evil that had possessed Bret. Throughout the gospels, we find Jesus releasing people from the power of these fallen angels.

> When evening came, many who were demon-possessed were brought to Him, and He drove out the spirits with a word and healed all the sick. (Matthew 8:16)
>
> When Jesus got out of the boat, a man with an evil spirit came from the tombs to meet Him. This man lived in the tombs, and no one could bind him any more, not even with a chain. For he had often been chained hand and foot, but he tore the chains apart and broke the irons on his feet. No one was strong enough to subdue him. Night and day among the tombs and in the hills he would cry out and cut himself with stones.
>
> When he saw Jesus from a distance, he ran and fell on his knees in front of him. He shouted at the top of his voice, "What do You want with me, Jesus, Son of the Most High God? Swear to God that You won't torture me!" For Jesus had said to him, "Come out of this man, you evil spirit!"

Then Jesus asked him, “What is your name?”

“My name is Legion,” he replied, “for we are many.” And he begged Jesus again and again not to send them out of the area.

A large herd of pigs was feeding on the nearby hillside. The demons begged Jesus, “Send us among the pigs; allow us to go into them.” He gave them permission, and the evil spirits came out and went into the pigs. The herd, about two thousand in number, rushed down the steep bank into the lake and were drowned.

Those tending the pigs ran off and reported this in the town and countryside, and the people went out to see what had happened. When they came to Jesus, they saw the man who had been possessed by the legion of demons, sitting there, dressed and in his right mind; and they were afraid. Those who had seen it told the people what had happened to the demon-possessed man—and told about the pigs as well. (Mark 5:2-16)

In the synagogue there was a man possessed by a demon, an evil spirit. He cried out at the top of his voice, “Ha! What do You want with us, Jesus of Nazareth? Have You come to destroy us? I know who You are—the Holy One of God!” “Be quiet!” Jesus said sternly. “Come out of him!” Then the demon threw the man down before them all and came out without injuring him. (Luke 4:33-35)

Each of these accounts reveals that Christ has *complete power* over demons. They bow down before Him (Mark 5:6), admit that He is God (Mark 5:7; James 2:19b), and obey Him (Matthew 8:16). With Christ in your life, you don't have to fear demons.

Are there really exorcisms to cast out demons?

The Bible doesn't include any ritual to cast out demons. Jesus simply tells the demons to get out. He instructs His disciples to use His name, along with prayer and fasting, to demand the demons vacate the premises. However, Jesus warns, merely "casting out" demons is not enough.

> "When an evil spirit comes out of a man, it goes through arid places seeking rest and does not find it. Then it says, 'I will return to the house I left.' When it arrives, it finds the house unoccupied, swept clean and put in order. Then it goes and takes with it seven other spirits more wicked than itself, and they go in and live there. And the final condition of that man is worse than the first. That is how it will be with this wicked generation." (Matthew 12:43-45)

As I told Tina, "Your mom has probably been listening to someone whose entire ministry consists of preaching against Satan. Don't get me wrong, Tina. Last week taught me that we need to talk in youth group about Satan's power and activities—and soon.

“But if we spent all our time in youth meetings talking about Satan, the occult, satanic lyrics, and demons, we’d be taking our attention off Christ. I wonder if Satan is just as content with demon *obsession* as he is with demon possession?”

“You know, now that you mention it, Mom’s been watching that preacher on TV who’s always casting out ‘foul spirits’ of someone or something,” Tina remarked. “And she’s bought a bunch of his tapes and books.”

“Satan is **subtle**. He can cause even sincere Christians to take their focus off Christ’s power and to direct it to his,” I said. “And that creates the kind of fear that grips your mom. The enemy is powerful, but we need to remember that ‘the one [Jesus] who is in you is greater than the one [Satan] who is in the world.’”[37]

“Thanks, Jim. Oh, could you give me a ride home? Our car’s in the garage with a clogged-up carburetor or something. But it’s not demons.”

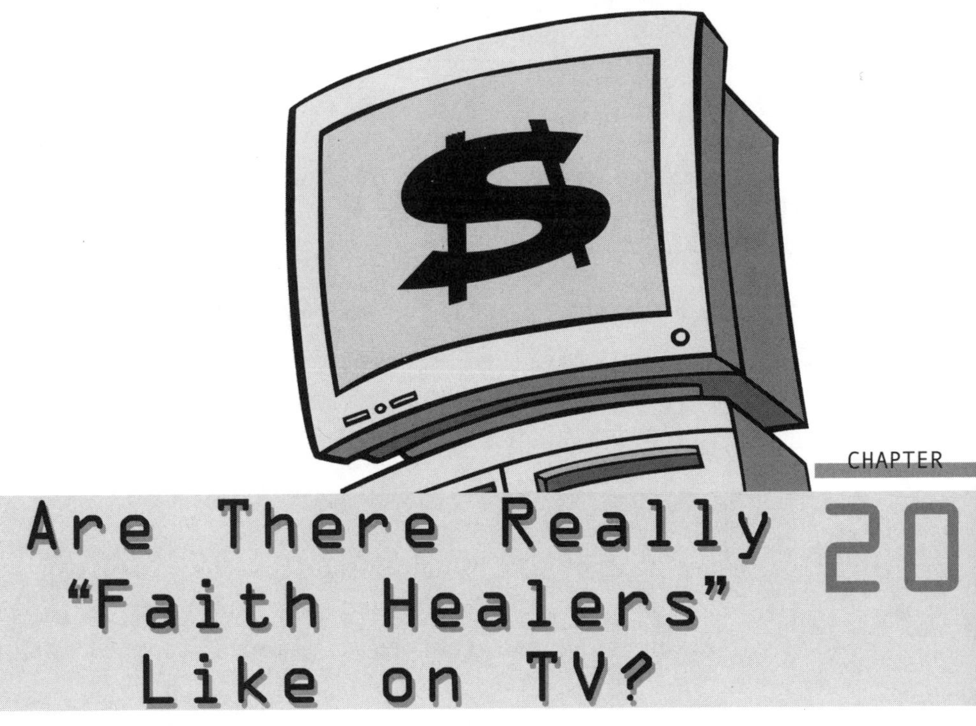

CHAPTER 20

Are There Really "Faith Healers" Like on TV?

"Jeeeee-sus doesn't want you sick!" The TV evangelist nearly pokes his index finger through the camera lens. "When the devil comes to your door with disease, you just reeeee-buke him in the name of Jeeeee-sus and the foul spirits will fa-leeeee!"

The theme music begins to play as the camera moves in for a close-up. "So, fa-riends, if you want to be free from each and every illness, write today. And for a donation of just $20, I'll send you my latest book ..."

I quickly change the channel and reach for another glass of **orange juice** and a handful of tissues. I wish getting over a cold was as simple as commanding, "Come out, foul spirits of post-nasal drip!"

Yet as I study God's Word, I am compelled to believe in divine healing:

> [The Lord] forgives all your sins and heals all your diseases. (Psalm 103:3)
>
> There some people brought to Him a man who was deaf and could hardly talk, and they begged Him to place His hand on the man. After He took him aside, away from the crowd, Jesus put His fingers into the man's ears. Then He spit and touched the man's tongue. He looked up to heaven and with a deep sigh said to him, "Ephphatha!" (which means, "Be opened!"). At this, the man's ears were opened, his tongue was loosened and he began to speak plainly. Jesus commanded them not to tell anyone. (Mark 7:32-36)

But as I study God's Word, I also become more and more suspicious of some faith healers' messages and methods.

1. *I'm suspicious of those who are constantly casting out demons of asthma, blindness, cancer, diabetes, and the rest of the anatomical alphabet.*

Romans 8:20–21 clearly points out that illness in general is a result of the fall and the human sin condition. But Matthew 4:24, 10:1, and 10:8 reveal that individual **illnesses** are not satanically inspired. Jesus' words to His disciples make a clear distinction between diseases and demon activity.

Why doesn't God heal all believers' diseases?

2. I'm suspicious of those who promise healing for every disease.

The apostle Paul definitely had the gift of healing. Acts 19:11 records that "God did extraordinary miracles through Paul, so that even handkerchiefs and aprons that had touched him were taken to the sick, and their illnesses were cured and the evil spirits left them." Acts 20:7–12 tells us he even raised the dead!

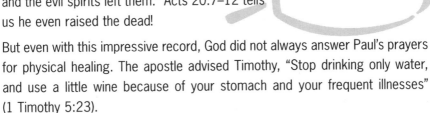

But even with this impressive record, God did not always answer Paul's prayers for physical healing. The apostle advised Timothy, "Stop drinking only water, and use a little wine because of your stomach and your frequent illnesses" (1 Timothy 5:23).

In 2 Timothy 4:20 we read that Paul "left Trophimus sick in Miletus." And his three prayers asking God to remove his own "thorn in the flesh" were not answered with physical healing (2 Corinthians 12:7–10).

3. I'm suspicious of those who make healing the focus of their public ministry.

Thirty-seven accounts of healing are detailed in the gospels and Acts. Only 10 occurred with a crowd present. Twelve occurred in small groups and 15 in private settings.

Rarely today do we hear those healing in Christ's name use His admonition: "Don't tell anyone!" Instead, we have weekly television programs featuring healing services and monthly mailings with a plague of pictures of the "healer" in action.

When God heals someone He does so to point people to Himself, not to draw attention to a human being. For example, Moses' leprous hand was healed not to impress the Israelites, but "... so that they may believe that the LORD ... has appeared to you" (Exodus 4:5). And Jesus told the Jews who did not believe He was God's Son: "Even though you do not believe Me, believe the miracles, that you may know and understand that the Father is in Me, and I in the Father" (John 10:38).

The apostle John writes that the purpose of recording the miracles of Jesus is "that you may believe that Jesus is the Christ, the Son of God, and that by believing you may have life in His name" (John 20:31).

If my healing will draw attention to God and advance His kingdom, then He will heal me. But if, like Paul, God can be glorified in me through emotional and spiritual—but not bodily—healing, He may choose not to heal me physically. Regardless, it is His kingdom's advancement that is the focus.

4. I'm suspicious of those who use healing as a fundraiser.

There is not one account in the gospels or the book of Acts of any money being exchanged or donated during a healing. Yet, recently, a famous faith healer boasted of making five million dollars annually from his healing "ministry."

Instead, when Simon, a recent convert and ex-sorcerer, asked to "buy" the Holy Spirit's power to work miracles, Peter shouts, "May your money perish with you, because you thought you could buy the gift of God with money! You have no part or share in this ministry, because your heart is not right before God" (Acts 8:20–21).

5. Finally, I'm suspicious of those who belittle medical treatment.

God has given us wisdom to understand these "fearfully and wonderfully made" bodies. We ought to treat our bodies well with the **medical knowledge** our world possesses and take advantage of the medical treatments available to us.

If God chooses to work miraculously to heal an individual, it can be humanly verified. Often, when Jesus healed leprosy and other diseases, He ordered those who had been healed to go the priests—who served as the public health officers of the day—to have the healing verified.

So if you believe you have been healed, do not make any changes in your activities or medications until a doctor can verify the healing. Unfortunately, there are tales of diabetics who felt they had been cured, ate a chocolate cake to celebrate the "miracle," and immediately went into a near-fatal insulin coma.

Let's review: There are *fake* healers.

Some "heal" actors from the audience. Some have mastered psychological techniques to make people believe they have been healed. Psychic healers, particularly in the Philippines, claim to be empowered by the Holy Spirit to remove diseased tissue without anesthesia, surgical tools, or any particular concern with infection. The "Amazing" Randi, however, has shown how this is always accomplished with sleight of hand—and plenty of chicken innards.

Others use the victim's normal remission of disease as "proof" of their healing powers. Some may even perform real "miracles" using satanic power. Matthew 24:24 warns that "false Christs and false prophets will appear and perform great signs and miracles to deceive even the elect—if that were possible."

But the Holy Spirit will help us discern those who are using human or satanic powers to accomplish "healings" with two simple questions.

1. **Who's getting the blame for the illness? If "demons" are the only cause the "healer" accepts, he or she is probably not legitimate.**
2. **Who's getting the credit for the healing? From the infertile, 90-year-old Sarah giving birth to Isaac to the dead who are raised in the book of Revelation, God the Savior is the focus—not the "healer" or the "healed."**

We do serve a God who continues to perform miracles.

And my cold? It's much better, thank you.

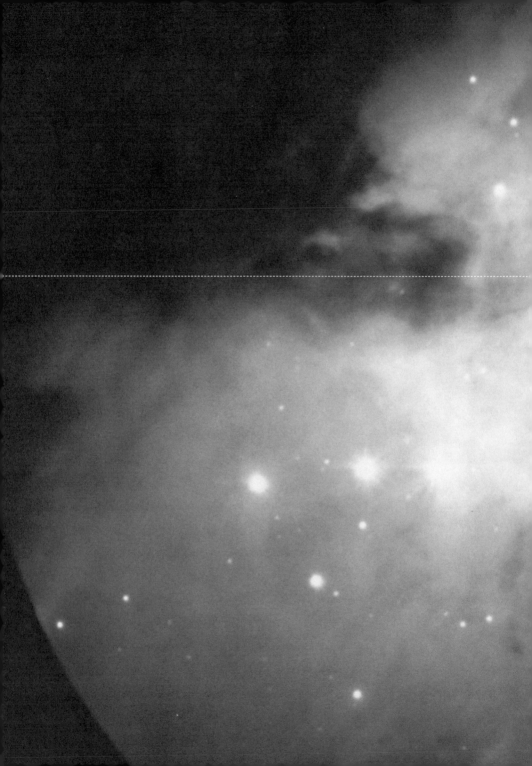

Part THREE

How Can You Keep from Being Deceived?

I have in my right hand, direct from my home office, today's Top Ten list:

You may be involved in a cult if ...

10. The signboard reads: **The Authentic Fellowship of the One and Only Real Truth. MEMBERS ONLY!**

CHAPTER

21 How Can You Know if Something Supernatural Is Just a Cult?

9. There are no "**Exit**" signs.
8. Members are not allowed to phone home.
7. The Authentic Fellowship of the One and Only Real Truth van has a gun rack.
6. Instead of taking your offering, the group takes your offspring.
5. Refreshments feature red Kool-Aid.
4. The leader demands that members refer to him as "**Grand Exalted Lord and Ruler**."

3. The choir robes have hoods.
2. The Grand Exalted Lord and Ruler's lecture notes have been canonized as "scripture."

And the number one sign you may be involved in a cult ...

1. The cross is on fire.

There's nothing funny about the increase in cult membership and the number of deaths resulting from these groups' bizarre beliefs. More than 900 followers of Jim Jones died by drinking poisoned Kool-Aid. Eighty-six Branch Davidians—25 of whom were children—died in the flames of David Koresh's Waco compound. Thirty-nine members of Marshall Applewhite's "Heaven's Gate" committed suicide, hoping to leave their "containers" to rendezvous with aliens traveling behind the Hale-Bopp comet.

While Koresh's apocalyptic prophecy teachings and Applewhite's alien messages seem worlds apart, most cults share common characteristics.

The group believes that it—and only it—knows the truth.

If a group claims only it knows the *true* truth or that members will be the sole survivors of some kind of cosmic calamity, it may be a cult. The Heaven's Gate group believed that only its members would escape earth's destruction. Jehovah's Witnesses believe that only they will be saved following the destruction of the world described in the Bible.

Some groups have their own "scripture" apart from or in addition to what orthodox Christians believe to be God's inspired Word. Christian Scientists have Mary Baker Eddy's *Science and Health,* which claims that "Jesus was the offspring of Mary's self-conscious communion with God." The Jehovah's Witnesses' *New World Translation* rewrites the Old and New Testaments to fit this cult's theology that only its members will be saved at the end of the world. Mormons have several additional books, including *The Book of Mormon,* which is believed to be translated from gold plates, and *Doctrines and Covenants,* which is based on founder Joseph Smith's visions.

Some more traditional religious groups also have **extra-biblical documents**.

The Seventh Day Adventists elevate the writings of founder, Ellen White, to "an authoritative source of truth," which "are not subject to criticism." The Roman Catholic Church teaches that the pope's *ex cathedra* pronouncements are "infallibly true" and "must be obediently accepted."

With so many groups claiming to have a corner on truth and interpretation of Scripture, it's important to believe the Bible is completely true in all it says.

Group members are isolated from family and former friends.

Cult leaders use peer pressure and paranoia to isolate members from the "outside" world. According to Mark Muesse, professor of religious studies at Rhodes College in Memphis, Tennessee, "Such groups tend to attract individuals who share their sense of isolation from the rest of society, who are struggling with a sense of identity or purpose in life."

The cult creates a sense of "us" against "them" that strengthens the **bond** among members—and the paranoia. The Branch Davidians seemed to have embraced Koresh's delusions by stockpiling food and weapons at their Waco "compound."

David Reed, professor of pastoral theology at Wycliff College at the University of Toronto, believes peoples' fear, insecurity, and loneliness are exploited by cult recruiters.

> ***Members are attracted to the cult by friendship and communal embrace. The one event in our lives that is most fearful is death. It can be seen as an attractive option to die communally and ritually ... as seems to have happened in California.***[38]

But for mass suicides to occur, Reed explains "individuals in the group must first have had their previous world—with relatives and friends—dismantled so that no attachment to the real world remains."[39]

The group's leader believes he or she knows what is best for individual members.

Because the founder of the cult is seen as the channel through which "God"—or an alien—has revealed the truth, there can be no questioning of his or her leadership and directives. The threat of being *excommunicated* from the only source of salvation keeps members under the oppressive power of the leader.

This absolute power and knowledge—with no accountability—often leads to tragic consequences!

Cults tend to be emotionally and, sometimes, physically and sexually abusive.

Cults often put recruits through a grueling indoctrination period. Kevin Crawley of the University of Iowa lists these common "indoctrination techniques to recruit and maintain members into a totalist ideology."

- Subjection to stress and fatigue
- Social disruption, isolation, and pressure
- Self-criticism and humiliation
- Fear, anxiety, and paranoia
- Control of information
- Escalating commitment
- Use of auto-hypnotism to induce "peak" experiences[40]

Once the recruit has been mentally and emotionally dominated by the leader or group, physical and even sexual abuse may follow. Mo David, of the 1960s cult Children of God, encouraged his female members to recruit new members by being "flirty fishers" who offered sex in exchange for attendance at his teaching sessions. Both Jim Jones and David Koresh believed that by having sex with their female followers, they would become more like Christ! (Koresh allegedly had sex with young girls as part of initiation rites.) Six of the dead Heaven's Gate members, including Applewhite, had submitted to surgery to remove their genitals as a part of the group's dogma against sexual differences.

Often, cult members are required to work long hours recruiting members and raising money for the cult. The motivation for slavish labor is usually a salvation-by-works mentality. Jehovah's Witnesses believe their salvation is, in part, assured by witnessing door to door.

"Christian" cults have a distorted view of Christ.

Just because a cult claims to be "Christian" doesn't mean it's following the genuine Christ. (We talked about this in chapter 12.)

What makes a cult a cult?

Some cultish characteristics creep into all social groups from business to education to organized religion. Maybe you've had a power-hungry, emotionally abusive boss or a know-it-all teacher. Coaches can become emotionally and physically **abusive** to their players. The Roman Catholic Church teaches that it is "the one true Church." So are they *cults*?

The *degree* and *number of ways* the group **deviates** from what is the orthodox faith (the established or accepted beliefs) determines whether the group is a cult. Denominations often differ on the finer points of theology, but most believe Jesus is divine and their earthly leaders are not. Big business tries to conform its workers into a "corporate culture" that controls employees' dress and thinking. Amway and other multilevel marketing companies often exhibit cult-like characteristics. But are they *cults*?

Anytime an organization attempts to control information and manipulate behavior, as well as isolate members from former family and friends, one should be concerned! The most telling clue, however, is the leader's refusal to be accountable to anyone except his vision of God, alien messengers, whoever or whatever. When a leader feels he or she is no longer accountable to anyone else in doctrine and behavior, the movement is moving toward **cult status**. Jim Jones began his ministry as a member of an evangelical denomination. Marshall Applewhite was the son of a mainline denomination pastor and attended a seminary. At some point, these two men became their own authorities, rejecting both human accountability and biblical truth.

Jesus predicted that false prophets and false religions would increase (Matthew 25:10–11), but He also taught,

> "I am sending you out like sheep among wolves. Therefore be shrewd as snakes and innocent as dove."
> (Matthew 10:16)

There are lots of supernatural leaders and groups in our world today.

Make sure you check them out using God's Word. If they contradict the Bible in any way, stay away!

Season Finale

Thanks for sharing this time with me. I trust you've found *The Why Files* helpful and informative. (I know I've learned more than I ever wanted to know about feminine hygiene products, embalmings, and alien abductions!)

Obviously, I've not answered all your questions on dating, death, and the supernatural. If I did that, you wouldn't buy any of the other books I've written—and we wouldn't want that to happen! (And if these three sell well, sequels will be on the way.)

Most of all, I hope you've discovered that God is interested in all areas of our lives. In His love, He equips and enables us to live lives that are "good, pleasing, and perfect" in this world (Romans 12:1–2).

I love hearing from readers, so please write me c/o Concordia Publishing House, Book Development Department, 3558 South Jefferson Avenue, Saint Louis, MO 63118-3968 or e-mail me at whyfiles@jameswatkins.com.

And stop by my website for links to the resources mentioned in this book series. There are also additional resources and up-to-the-minute information on sex, death, and the supernatural at: www.jameswatkins.com. (Click on the Book Updates link on my home page.)

Again, thanks for taking the time to read this book. And do tell all your friends about the series. Until we share another book together ...

"Dear friend, I pray that you may enjoy good health and that all may go well with you, even as your soul is getting along well" (3 John 2).

Jim Watkins

How Do I Reach My Friend Who Is into All Kinds of Supernatural Things?

"You can't reach New Agers through any of the normal ways Christians try to reach out and touch them," Gail Ow, a former New Age believer, claims.

> ***One person asked me if I [knew] Jesus Christ as my Lord and Savior and I said, "Sure!" But I didn't even have a concept of a "Savior" because New Agers believe all people are good. And I didn't need a "Lord" because I was self-reliant. I was very successful in my career, had a husband, two children, a maid and nanny, and the whole thing. I was so proud of myself and my intelligence, I wasn't willing to accept that anyone had anything over me. Besides, Christians were all weird to me. They were going to get me into some Kool-Aid cult, brainwash me, and take me away.***

Gail has been a Christian for 18 months now and is actively seeking ways to share her new faith with former New Agers. But it is a challenge.

"When people tried to witness to me, nothing they said touched my heart. I'd tell them, 'You think you know the *truth*, well I do too! Okay we're done, let's go on to something else.' "

So how do you reach the 38 million Americans who believe in reincarnation, "human potential," and other New Age beliefs?

Point Out Inconsistent "Truth"

Sylvia Herrera, a Christian and speaker to women's groups, believes that New Age beliefs begin to crumble when exposed to the harsh light of truth and the Holy Bible.

> **I started out as a Christian but didn't [really believe in Christ as my Savior]. As a teenager, I floundered around and became involved in Job's Daughter [a division of the Masonic Lodge, which is based on Egyptian worship]. As an adult, I became involved in astrology, Ouija boards, tarot cards, psychics, Shirley MacLaine's books, and finally married a Mormon. The Mormons had answers for everything but I wasn't knowledgeable enough to counteract it. But there was something in the back of my mind that there was something wrong with it, but I really didn't know. Through Ex-Mormons for Jesus literature, I began to put it all together and Mormon beliefs just began to fall apart.**

Many New Agers who have converted to Christianity point out the inconsistency in the New Age "doctrines." And like Sylvia's faith in Mormonism, the contradictions begin to erode confidence.

For instance, Edgar Cayce, the father of American reincarnation, reveals major contradictions in his teachings. Cayce believed that Jesus Christ was actually Adam and Enoch in a reincarnated state. That would be an impossibility since Adam and Enoch were both alive at the same time. His own reincarnated history revealed inconsistencies. Cayce taught the Western version of reincarnation that people only become better and better after repeated reincarnations. Yet he also claimed to have been the prophet Lucius of Judea who was reincarnated as an immoral Frenchman determined to "indulge his sexual appetites" and a Virginia colonist with numerous illegitimate children.

And if people are reincarnated as better and better, why are crime rates, abuse statistics, and divorce filings continuing to increase?

Shirley MacLaine, the modern prophet of New Age-ism, is also inconsistent—and inaccurate—in her teachings. For instance, the best-selling author claims Jesus taught, "As you sow, so shall you reap." Jesus is not recorded teaching this; rather the apostle Paul. MacLaine also claims that Scripture taught reincarnation but the Council of Nicea in A.D. 553 deleted all mention of it. The council actually met in A.D. 325 and dealt with the question of the formation of souls, not reincarnation. Surely, someone in touch with "universal wisdom" should be more accurate!

Sylvia continues, "As I began reading information from the Ex-Mormons for Jesus, I discovered all the incorrect prophecies of Joseph Smith and the unbelievable teachings of Brigham Young, such as men living on the moon who were about four feet tall."

Indeed, "You shall know the truth and the truth shall set you free."

Point Out Empty "Promises"

Gail's faith in the New Age began to waiver when she actually began to fulfill her goals.

> Although I was rich and successful, I felt so very empty. I had reached my "human potential" and I still didn't feel better. I got mad at God and shouted, "Why is it that I'm the only one out there making all this money and can't be happy with what I'm doing?"
>
> But I did cry out to God to take this emptiness away and to take anything out of my life that would keep me from believing Him. And so God spent the next three or four years pouring junk out of my life—my overdependence on money and the men in my life. God had to break me to get me to the point where I believed I couldn't do it by myself. My marriage and life just fell apart. I got a divorce, quit work, closed my door, unplugged the phone, and just crawled into a cocoon. I was just two days away from a mental hospital.
>
> Here I was an unemployed, single mother of two. When I would call my New Age friends and explain my situation they'd say, "Oh, golly," and hang up the phone. But when I talked to my Christian friends—and they all thought I was a Christian—they would simply say, "Get into His Word," which didn't mean a thing to me. But I got to the point where I was literally on my knees crying out, "God, save me."

Point Out "Cut and Paste" Scripture

Gail's eventual conversion to Christianity came as a result of studying God's Word.

> Even though I was deep into the New Age, I had this indescribable desire to read the Bible. I wanted to find God, but I didn't trust Christians enough to talk to any of them.
>
> New Agers know bits and pieces of Scripture. I would hear the promises of Matthew 6 about God clothing the lilies of the fields and feeding the birds, but nothing about "seek first His kingdom." I've seen posters with Isaiah's promise of running and not being weary, but not a word about God judging false prophets. Quoting Scripture to New Agers is like, "Yeah, yeah, I've heard that." The secret to reaching them is to encourage them to study the Bible complete[ly].

Studying God's Word also was the turning point for Sylvia.

> I think in the back of my mind, I still had my Christian roots. God says His Word doesn't come back void.
>
> But the thing that really got to me was God's Word, especially in Isaiah 44:6: "I am the first and I am the last; apart from Me there is no God." I was really hungry and searching, and just began studying the Bible. [I confessed my faith in Jesus] and felt an oppressiveness leave me as I cleaned out the house of Mormon literature and astrology.

Pam Stephens, a Christian speaker and associate of Florence Littauer, also attributes to Scripture her salvation from astrology.[41]

> I became a Christian at age 9 and went through confirmation classes, but was really not well grounded. After marriage, dropping out of church, and becoming a stay-at-home parent in a rural area, I had to find something to fill up my time. I began reading horoscope books and that dabbling became more and more intense until I finally had three full bookshelves of astrology books and started to chart my own horoscopes.
>
> But one day I took a very dusty book off the shelf—which happened to be God's Word—and opened it up to Deuteronomy 18:10-12, which condemns all forms of the occult. I honestly hadn't thought there was anything wrong with combining Christianity and astrology. I had never heard that. But I knew in my heart that if God said it was wrong, I either had to agree with Him and accept that, or I had to completely give up calling myself a believer. I knew He was God, but I didn't realize He was a jealous God. I confessed it as sin and that day I burned all my astrology books in the fireplace. It wasn't until years later that I read of the same kind of bonfire in Acts 19:19.

Pam doesn't believe there is a "formula" for leading New Agers to Christ.

> It was the loving concern from the heart of my Christian friends. Christians need to build relationships with New Agers and establish a right to be heard as well as living the Christian life before them. That gives us credibility. But the most important factor is

the prayer that the "scales will be dropped" from their eyes that blind them to what real truth is. Satan's receptions are empty promises, but God brings fulfillment to all His promises through His Son, Jesus.

Gail, Pam, and Sylvia all agree it was the prayers of family and friends, as well as God's Word empowered by His Holy Spirit, that finally convinced them of the truth of Christianity.

Endnotes

1. I'm not implying that UFOs are "chariots of the gods" or angelic spacecraft as some have speculated. Rather, to Ezekiel, this was an unidentified flying object!
2. Quoted by Bernard D. Gildenberg and David E. Thomas in "Case Closed: Reflections on the 1997 Air Force Roswell Report," *The Skeptical Inquirer* (May/June 1998), 32-33.
3. Gildenberg and Thomas, 33.
4. Susan Blackmore, "Abduction by Aliens or Sleep Paralysis?" *The Skeptical Inquirer* (May/June 1998), 24.
5. Robert A. Baker, "The Aliens Among Us: Hypnotic Regression Revisited." *The Skeptical Inquirer* (12:2), 147-162.
6. Blackmore, 24.
7. Alan Hale, "An Astronomer's Personal Statement on UFOs," *The Skeptical Inquirer* (March 1997, online edition).
8. The various explanations and characteristics of witches and witchcraft in this section were gleaned from Laurie Cabot, *Power of the Witch* (New York, New York: Delacourt Press, Dell Publishing, 1989).
9. Dolphin's controversial theory is critiqued by Cecil Adams' Straight Dope Website at www.straightdope.com/columns/990507.html.

10. Daniel Cohen, *The Encyclopedia of Ghosts* (New York, New York: Dorset Press, 1984), 202.

11. Danny Korem and Paul Meier, *The Fakers: Exploding the Myths of the Supernatural* (Old Tappan, New Jersey: Fleming H. Revell Company, 1980), 101.

12. A drachma was about one day's wage. (At today's minimum wage of $5.25 an hour, that's a total of $2 million!)

13. Korem and Meier, 69.

14. Korem and Meier, 72.

15. C. S. Lewis, *Mere Christianity* (New York, New York: Macmillan, 1964), 40-41.

16. Stoner's unbelievable odds were verified as accurate by the executive council of the American Scientific Affiliation.

17. Wilbur M. Smith, *Therefore Stand: Christian Apologetics* (Grand Rapids, Michigan: Kregel Publications, 1965), 386.

18. Francis A. Schaeffer and C. Everett Koop, *Whatever Happened to the Human Race* (Old Tappan, New Jersey: Fleming H. Revell Company, 1979), 159-160.

19. Josh McDowell, *Evidence That Demands a Verdict* (San Bernadino, California: Campus Crusade for Christ, Inc., 1972), 2.

20. Sir Frederick Kenyon, *The Bible and Archaeology* (New York, New York: Harper and Row, 1940), 288.

21. Robert Dick Wilson, "What Is an Expert?" *The Bible League Quarterly* (1955).

22. Josh McDowell, *More Than a Carpenter* (Wheaton, Illinois: Tyndale House Publishers, Inc., 1977), 73.

23. Walter Wagner, *Heavenly Humor for All God's Children* (Old Tappan, New Jersey: Fleming H. Revell Company, 1975) 54.

24. H. Orton Wiley and Paul T. Culbertson, *Introduction to Christian Theology* (Kansas City, Missouri: Beacon Hill Press, 1946), 83.

25. John Gilchrist, "The Love of God in the Qur'an and the Bible," online at www.answering—islam .org/Gilchrest/love.html

26. Walda Woods, from her website at http:// certificate.net/wwio/, copyright 1998.

27. From Deepak Chopra's official website at www.chopra.com.

28. Shirley MacLaine, *Out on a Limb (*New York, New York: Bantam, 1983), 214.

29. MacLaine, 352.

30. MacLaine, 352.

31. James Redfield, *The Celestine Prophecy* (New York, New York: Warner Books, 1997). This novel follows a man who "goes on a journey of self-discovery attempting to retrieve an ancient Peruvian manuscript full of insights into life and spirituality, in a powerful and revelatory fable." The ninth "step" in this pilgrimage is to "evolve beyond this plane [and] connect to God's energy in such a way that we will eventually became beings of light and walk straight into heaven."

32. *A Brief Statement of the Doctrinal Position of the Missouri Synod* (St. Louis, Missouri: Concordia Publishing House, 1932).

33. Edward W.A. Koehler, *A Summary of Christian Doctrine* (St. Louis, Missouri: Concordia Publishing House, 1939, 1952), 32.

34. Norman L. Geisler and Ronald M. Brooks, *When Skeptics Ask* (Wheaton, Illinois: Scripture Press Publications, Inc., 1990), 76.

35. Anita Belk, "Touched by an Angel," Angel Haven Website at www2.angelhaven.com/stories/story_Touched.asp.

36. Read this whole chapter (Daniel 10) to have a clearer picture of Daniel's vision. In verse 13, he's talking about a demonically inspired attempt to use the kingdom of Persia to thwart God's plan for His people. The attempt failed when Michael came to the help of the angel clothed in linen (verse 5).

37. See 1 John 4:4.

38. David Reed, Apologetics Research Resources on Religious Cults, Sects, Movements, Doctrines, Etc., online at www.gospelcom.net/apologeticsindex/index.html.

39. Reed.

40. Kevin Crawley, alt.mindcontrol newsgroup response, "A Behavioral Definition," May 28, 1994, at http://ex-cult.org/General/cult.definition.

41. Visit Pam Stephen's website at http://hometown.aol.com//psstephens.

Index